Bend, Don't Break: Finding Your Way Back to Abundance

Copyright © 2024 Dr. Constance Santego

Copy Editor and Interior Design: Constance Santego
Book Layout: ©2017 BookDesignTemplates.com

Ordering Information:
Quantity sales. Special discounts are available on quantity purchases by corporations, associations, and others. For details, contact the "Special Sales Department" at the address above.

Trade paperback ISBN: 978-1-990062-18-6

eBook ISBN 978-1-990062-19-3

Created and published In Canada. Printed and bound in the United States of America

Published by Maximillian Enterprises
Kelowna, BC
Canada
www.constancesantego.ca

BEND, DON'T BREAK:

Finding Your Way Back to Abundance

ALSO BY DR. CONSTANCE SANTEGO

FICTION

THE NINE SPIRITUAL GIFTS SERIES:

Journey of a Soul – (Vol. 1 Michael)

Language of a Soul – (Vol. 2 Gabriel)

Prophecy of a Soul – (Vol. 3 Bath Kol)

Healing of a Soul – (Vol. 4 Raphael)

Miracles of a Soul – (Vol. 5 Hamied)

NON-FICTION

The Intuitive Life, The Gift of Prophecy, Third Edition

Your Persona... The Mask You Wear

Angelic Lifestyle, A Vibrant Lifestyle

Angelic Lifestyle 42-Day Energy Cleanse

Archangel Michael's Soul Retrieval Guide

Tesla and the Future of Energy Medicine

SECRETS OF A HEALER, SERIES:

Magic of Aromatherapy (Vol. I)

Magic of Reflexology (Vol. II)

Magic of The Gifts (Vol. III)

Magic of Muscle Testing (Vol. IV)

Magic of Iridology (Vol. V)

Magic of Massage (Vol. VI)

Magic of Hypnotherapy (Vol. VII)

Magic of Reiki (Vol. VIII)

Magic of Advanced Aromatherapy (Vol. IX)

Magic of Esthetics (Vol. X)

FOR CHILDREN

I am Big Tonight. I Don't Need the Light!

BEND, DON'T BREAK:

Finding Your Way Back to Abundance

DR. CONSTANCE SANTEGO

Maximillian Enterprises inc

DEDICATION

I would like to dedicate this book to

God, the Universe, and

the Law of Attraction

PREFACE

Welcome to "Bend, Don't Break: Finding Your Way Back to Abundance." In the pages that follow, we embark on a journey of transformation, resilience, and discovery—a path inspired by the graceful strength of the bamboo tree. My fascination with bamboo began not just with its physical properties but with what it symbolizes: resilience, growth, and the ability to thrive amidst the challenges life throws our way.

The Essence of Bamboo

Across cultures, the bamboo tree is celebrated for its unique combination of strength and flexibility. Its capacity to bend without breaking under the fiercest winds is a profound metaphor for life's trials. This book draws on that metaphor, aiming to show you how, like the bamboo, you can stand strong, bend with change, and continue to grow and flourish.

Dr. Constance Santego x

Bamboo teaches us about the power of adaptability. In our quest for abundance, we'll face unforeseen changes and challenges. It's our flexibility in the face of these changes, much like the bamboo bending in the wind, that enables us to emerge unscathed, sometimes even stronger than before.

Prosperity and Luck

Bamboo is also a symbol of prosperity and good fortune. This book weaves the principle of positivity—central to the cultivation of good fortune—into the fabric of its message. A positive mindset and environment act as fertile ground from which our deepest desires can manifest into reality.

Growth and Renewal

Remarkably, bamboo is among the fastest-growing plants in the world. This rapid growth symbolizes our potential for swift transformation and renewal. Through the lessons contained in this book, you'll discover how your desires can manifest rapidly, underpinned by belief, intention, and action, mirroring bamboo's growth.

Persistence and Environmental Harmony

Manifestation is a journey of persistence and aligning with our environment. Like bamboo, which contributes positively to its ecosystem, our manifestations should harmonize with the world around us, benefiting not only ourselves but also those we share our world with.

In Closing

The metaphor of the bamboo tree serves as our guiding light in "Bend, Don't Break." Its lessons on resilience, positivity, and growth are integral to finding your way back to abundance. As we navigate this journey together, let the bamboo inspire us to embrace change, cultivate a positive mindset, and align our actions with our deepest goals. Here's to bending with the challenges, not breaking under pressure, and flourishing in our pursuit of abundance.

Thank you for joining me on this journey.
Warmly, Connie

Contents

BEND, DON'T BREAK:

Finding Your Way Back to Abundance

BEND, DON'T BREAK

Resilience is the garden of the spirit,
where every hardship endured is a seed of growth,
blooming into abundance.

Part I – Introduction

Welcome to "Bend, Don't Break: Finding Your Way Back to Abundance."

This book is a testament to the unyielding strength of the human spirit and the boundless potential within you to manifest a life filled with abundance, joy, and fulfillment. At its heart, the journey of manifestation is a profound awakening—a realization that the power to shape your reality lies within your grasp.

The path you're about to embark upon is not just about acquiring material wealth or achieving surface-level desires. It's a deeper exploration of the Law of Attraction, a universal principle that teaches us how like attracts like and how our thoughts, emotions, and actions are inextricably linked to the fabric of our lives. Through the pages of this book, you will discover how to harness this law, not just as a tool for manifesting your desires but as a compass for navigating life's challenges and rediscovering your innate power.

Every journey has its share of obstacles, and it's natural to encounter moments when your path seems obscured, your resolve tested, and your spirit weary. "Bend, Don't Break" is about those moments. It's about recognizing that setbacks, detours, and even failures are not signs of weakness but opportunities for growth, transformation, and realignment with your true purpose.

We'll explore how emotional healing plays a crucial role in clearing the blockages that impede your ability to manifest. You'll learn practical actions to take when faced with setbacks and how to maintain your focus on abundance even when scarcity seems to cloud your vision. This book is a guide to finding your way back to your path whenever you feel lost, reminding you that bending under the weight of your challenges doesn't mean breaking.

Your journey begins with an acknowledgment of your own power—the power to change, to grow, and to manifest the life you've always dreamed of. As you turn these pages, you'll uncover the strategies and insights to help you navigate through the lows and soar to the highs, all the while keeping your eyes fixed on the horizon of abundance.

"Bend, Don't Break" is more than a book; it's a companion on your journey to rediscovering how resilient, powerful, and capable you truly are. Let's embark on this journey together, with open hearts and minds, ready to embrace the abundance that awaits us.

As you embark on this journey with "Bend, Don't Break: Finding Your Way Back to Abundance," it's crucial to grasp the essence of what powers your path: the Law of Attraction. This universal principle is the backbone of manifestation, teaching us that like attracts like. Your thoughts, feelings, and beliefs aren't just passive reflections of your experience—they actively shape your reality. When you focus on what you truly desire and maintain a positive outlook, you set the stage for positive experiences to come your way. On the flip side, dwelling in negativity only serves to attract more of the same.

The journey of manifestation isn't about idle wishes; it demands your focused intention. It's about being crystal clear about your desires, painting them in vivid detail in your mind and heart. The universe is listening, but it responds best to clarity and precision. This clarity isn't just about knowing what you want—it's about believing in its possibility. Your belief is the foundation of your manifestation efforts. Without it, even the most fervent desires might fail to materialize.

Your emotional state is a powerful tool in this process. Think of your emotions as vibrational signals you're constantly sending out into the universe. Positive emotions such as joy, love, and gratitude can amplify your manifestation efforts, acting as magnets for your desires. But just as positive emotions can attract, negative emotions can repel.

Everything in the universe, including you and your thoughts, vibrates at a certain frequency. By elevating your vibrational frequency to match that of your desires, you align yourself more closely with them, making their manifestation in your life all the more likely. Techniques like meditation, affirmations, and visualization aren't just practices for relaxation—they're tools to help raise your vibrational state.

Remember, manifesting your desires isn't a one-off magic trick. It's a daily practice of aligning your thoughts, emotions, and actions with your goals. Whether it's through journaling your intentions, practicing gratitude, or visualizing your desired outcomes, each act reinforces your manifestation efforts.

It's easy to misconstrue manifestation as some mystical process that magically grants wishes without effort. However, true manifestation is about co-creating with the universe. It's a dance of taking intentional steps toward your goals while staying open and receptive to the opportunities and possibilities that the universe presents to you.

At its heart, the path of manifestation is a journey of self-discovery. It's an invitation to dive deep into your desires, to understand your true self, and to challenge and overcome the limiting beliefs that hold you back. This journey not only brings you closer to realizing your dreams but also fosters personal growth and development.

Understanding and applying the principles of the Law of Attraction empowers us to consciously shape our lives. By embracing these concepts, you can navigate through life's ebbs and flows with grace, transforming challenges into opportunities for growth and steering your life back to the abundance that awaits.

The Law of Attraction

The Law of Attraction is a philosophical concept suggesting that positive or negative thoughts bring positive or negative experiences into a person's life. This principle is based on the belief that people and their thoughts are made from "pure energy" and that a process of like energy attracting like energy exists through which a person can improve their health, wealth, and personal relationships.

Key Components of the Law of Attraction

- Thought Power: It emphasizes the power of our thoughts and how they shape our reality. The idea is that focusing on positive or negative thoughts can bring positive or negative experiences into one's life.
- Vibrational Match: According to this law, the universe responds to the vibrational energy you put out. This

means if you emit positivity, you attract positive situations and vice versa.

- Manifestation: This is the process through which the thoughts, focused energy, and intentions of a person materialize into reality. It suggests that by envisioning and believing in a desired outcome, one can influence its manifestation in the real world.

- Attraction through Visualization: Visualization is a crucial practice in the Law of Attraction, where individuals are encouraged to create a mental image of their desired outcome *as though it has already happened,* reinforcing their belief and intention.

- Gratitude and Positivity: Maintaining a state of gratitude and a positive outlook is believed to further attract positive changes and opportunities.

The Mechanism Behind the Manifestation of Complaints

The concept that "What we *bitch* about, we also manifest" highlights a crucial aspect of the Law of Attraction, emphasizing the power of our focus and how it shapes our reality. This principle suggests that when we spend our time complaining or focusing on negative aspects of our lives, we inadvertently attract more of those negative circumstances to us. It's based on the idea that the universe responds not just to our desires and positive affirmations but also to where we direct our energy and attention, including our complaints and grievances.

- Energy Follows Attention: Explains how our energy amplifies whatever we focus on. By consistently focusing on negative aspects, we increase their presence in our lives.
- Vibrational Match: Discusses how complaining lowers our vibrational frequency, making us a vibrational match for more negative experiences rather than positive ones.

- Reinforcement of Negative Beliefs: **Outlines how habitual complaining reinforces limiting beliefs and negative thought patterns, creating a cycle that's difficult to break and attracts more negativity.**

Transforming Complaints into Positive Manifestations

- Awareness and Mindfulness: **Emphasizes the importance of becoming aware of our complaint patterns and triggers. Mindfulness can help us catch ourselves in the act of complaining and choose a different response.**
- Reframing Perspectives: **Encourages the practice of reframing negative situations or aspects into learning opportunities or challenges to overcome. This change in perspective can shift the energy and focus toward more positive outcomes.**
- Gratitude as an Antidote: **Advocates for the practice of gratitude as a powerful tool to counteract complaining. By focusing on what we are thankful for, we shift our**

attention and energy to positivity, attracting more of it into our lives.

Practical Steps to Reduce Complaining

- Complaint-Free Challenges: **Proposes engaging in complaint-free challenges, where individuals consciously avoid complaining for a set period, replacing complaints with positive statements or solutions.**
- Journaling: **Suggests using a journal to track complaints and their triggers, as well as to document positive aspects and moments of gratitude. This can help shift focus away from negativity.**
- Developing a Solution-Oriented Mindset: **Encourages the cultivation of a mindset that looks for solutions rather than dwelling on problems. This proactive approach can significantly reduce the impulse to complain.**

The Power of Positive Expression

- Expressing Desires Positively: Highlights the importance of expressing desires and frustrations in a positive, constructive manner. Instead of focusing on what we don't want, we should articulate what we do want.

- Building Supportive Environments: Discusses the role of our social and environmental contexts in shaping our complaint patterns and offers advice on creating or seeking environments that encourage positivity and constructive communication.

What You Can Gain

This book is designed to be a compass and companion on your journey toward self-discovery and manifestation. Here, you will learn not just to dream but to transform those dreams into your lived reality. From understanding the basic tenets of the Law of Attraction to navigating the complex process of healing from trauma, this guide is a holistic approach to achieving a life of abundance, fulfillment, and joy.

You will be equipped with the tools and techniques to:

- Align your thoughts, emotions, and energy with your deepest desires
- Identify and release the traumas and blockages that hold you back
- Cultivate a mindset of abundance and positivity
- Manifest your dreams into reality through actionable steps

Embarking on Your Journey

As you turn these pages, you embark on the most crucial journey of all—the journey within. It's a path of discovering your limitless potential, healing your deepest wounds, and creating a life that resonates with your truest self. This book is your map, your guide, and your beacon of hope, illuminating the path toward a brighter, more abundant future.

Welcome to your journey.
It begins now.

Bend, Don'

An Awakening

An awakening in the context of manifestation is a profound realization or enlightenment that marks the beginning of one's journey toward understanding and harnessing the power within oneself to influence one's reality. This pivotal moment is characterized by a shift in perception, where individuals come to recognize their innate potential to co-create their experiences with the Universe through their thoughts, emotions, and actions.

Key Aspects of an Awakening

- Realization of Power: The individual realizes that they are not merely subject to the whims of fate but have the power to influence their outcomes. This understanding often comes with a sense of empowerment and responsibility.

- A Shift in Perspective: Awakening brings about a significant shift in how one views the world, themselves, and their place within the cosmos. There's a deeper understanding of the interconnectedness of all things and the role of energy and intention in shaping life experiences.

- Heightened Awareness: There's an increase in self-awareness and consciousness, allowing individuals to see beyond their previous limitations and beliefs. This heightened awareness helps identify and release negative patterns or beliefs that hinder growth and manifestation.

- Sense of Purpose and Alignment: Awakening often leads to a clearer sense of purpose and a desire to align one's life with one's true desires and highest good. It instigates a journey of self-discovery and personal development.

- Connection with the Universe: There's a deepened sense of connection with the Universe or a higher power, accompanied by trust in its guidance and support. This connection is crucial for co-creation and receiving insights or signs along the manifestation path.

Experiencing an Awakening

An awakening can be triggered by various experiences, such as profound personal challenges, introspection, meditation, or even seemingly random moments of insight. While the experience is deeply personal and can vary widely among individuals, it often leads to a transformative period of growth, healing, and empowerment.

Navigating Post-Awakening

The period following an awakening is critical for grounding the newfound insights into one's daily life. It involves:

- Integrating New Understandings: Actively incorporating the lessons and insights from the awakening into one's life, which may involve changing habits, beliefs, and relationships that no longer align with one's new understanding.

- Continued Exploration and Growth: Engaging in practices that promote further growth and understanding, such as meditation, journaling, reading, or seeking the guidance of mentors or like-minded communities.

- Practicing Co-creation: Beginning to actively co-create with the Universe by setting intentions, practicing visualization, and taking aligned actions toward manifesting one's desires.

An awakening is not an end but the beginning of a rich, ongoing journey of self-discovery, manifestation, and co-creation with the Universe. It opens up new possibilities and pathways for creating a life that truly reflects one's desires, values, and highest potential.

The Power of Mindset

The Power of Mindset chapter delves into the profound impact that one's mindset can have on one's ability to manifest desires, overcome challenges, and ultimately shape the trajectory of one's life. A mindset can be understood as a set of attitudes or fixed beliefs that one holds, which can either be limiting or empowering. This chapter explores how adopting a positive, growth-oriented mindset is crucial in harnessing the power of manifestation and achieving personal growth and fulfillment.

Key Concepts of Mindset in Manifestation:

- Growth vs. Fixed Mindset: Drawing on the work of psychologist Carol Dweck, this concept distinguishes between two primary types of mindsets—fixed and growth. A fixed mindset believes that abilities and outcomes are static and unchangeable, while a growth mindset embraces challenges, effort, and the potential for development. The chapter illustrates how a growth mindset is essential for effective manifestation.

- **Belief in Possibility:** The power of mindset begins with the belief in the possibility of achieving your desires. This belief acts as the foundation upon which intentions are set and actions are taken, influencing the vibrational energy you emit and attract.

- **Overcoming Limiting Beliefs:** Identifying and transforming limiting beliefs that stem from past experiences, societal conditioning, or self-doubt is crucial. These beliefs can act as barriers to manifestation, and changing them requires conscious effort and, sometimes, professional guidance.

- **Visualization and Affirmation:** Techniques such as visualization and affirmation are discussed as practical tools for reinforcing a positive mindset. Visualization involves creating a mental image of your desired outcome, while affirmations are positive statements repeated to embed empowering beliefs.

- **Resilience and Adaptability:** The chapter underscores the importance of resilience and adaptability in facing setbacks and obstacles. A powerful mindset is not deterred by failures but sees them as opportunities for learning and growth.

- Mindfulness and Presence: Incorporating mindfulness practices can enhance one's mindset by fostering presence, awareness, and acceptance of the current moment. This presence can reduce anxiety about the future or regrets about the past, aligning one more closely with their manifestation goals.

Application and Transformation

- Daily Practices: Suggests daily practices to cultivate a powerful mindset, including journaling, meditation, and gratitude exercises. These practices help maintain focus, clarity, and positivity.
- Real-Life Examples: Sharing real-life stories of individuals who have successfully shifted their mindset to overcome challenges and manifest their desires, providing inspiration and evidence of the power of mindset.
- Community and Support: Encourages building a supportive community or seeking mentors who embody the empowered mindset you aspire to. Surrounding yourself with positivity can significantly influence your mindset and manifestation abilities.

Major Life Stages

Major life stages often come with pivotal moments that prompt us to pivot, make changes to our plans, or shift paths. These stages can align with Erik Erikson's psychosocial stages of development, which outline key conflicts and potential resolutions from infancy through late adulthood. While the specific ages at which individuals experience these turning points can vary, here's a general overview of life stages where significant pivots often occur:

1. Adolescence (around 12-18 years): This stage is marked by the quest for identity versus confusion about one's role. Teenagers and young adults often make pivotal decisions about their education, career paths, and social identities.

2. Young Adulthood (around 19-40 years): In this phase, individuals face the challenge of forming intimate relationships versus isolation. Decisions about long-term partnerships, marriage, and starting a family often occur alongside career development and lifestyle choices.

3. Midlife (around 40-65 years): This period, often termed the "midlife crisis," involves reflection on life achievements and direction, leading to significant career changes, lifestyle adjustments, and sometimes, re-evaluation of relationships.

4. Retirement Age (65 years and older): As individuals enter retirement, they often reevaluate their purpose and contribution to society, leading to involvement in volunteer work, the pursuit of neglected passions, or mentorship roles.

Each of these stages comes with its own set of challenges and opportunities for growth. Recognizing these pivotal periods can help individuals navigate life transitions more smoothly, making informed decisions that align with their evolving goals and values.

Emotional Alchemy

Emotional Alchemy refers to the transformative process of turning negative, unproductive emotions into positive, constructive forces in our lives. This concept draws on the metaphor of alchemy—the medieval precursor to chemistry focused on turning base metals into gold—to describe the process of transforming the "base" material of our challenging emotions into "gold," or valuable insights and energy that propel us forward. Emotional Alchemy involves recognizing, understanding, and actively working with our emotions to change how we experience and react to different situations, ultimately leading to personal growth and improved well-being.

Key Components of Emotional Alchemy

- Awareness: The first step in emotional alchemy is becoming aware of your emotions. This involves acknowledging your feelings without judgment and understanding that emotions are temporary states that can be managed and transformed.

- Acceptance: **Accepting your emotions is crucial. It means recognizing that all emotions, even negative ones, are part of the human experience. Acceptance does not mean resignation but acknowledging your feelings as the first step toward transformation.**

- Understanding: **Delve into the roots of your emotions. Often, negative emotions stem from past experiences, fears, or deep-seated beliefs. By understanding the source of your emotions, you can begin to address and heal underlying issues.**

- Transformation: **This is the core of emotional alchemy—actively working to change how you interpret and react to your emotions. Techniques include reframing your perspective, employing mindfulness and meditation, and using your emotions as catalysts for positive change.**

- Integration: **The final step involves integrating your transformed emotions into your life. This means using the energy and insights gained from the process to foster personal growth, improve relationships, and enhance overall well-being.**

Techniques in Emotional Alchemy

- **Mindfulness and Meditation:** Practicing mindfulness allows you to observe your emotions without becoming overwhelmed by them. Meditation can help calm the mind, making it easier to work through emotions logically and compassionately.

- **Cognitive Reframing:** This technique involves changing your perspective on a situation to alter your emotional response to it. By reframing challenges as opportunities for growth, you can shift negative emotions to more positive or neutral feelings.

- **Breathwork:** Controlled breathing exercises can help manage emotional responses by calming the nervous system and reducing stress levels, creating a more balanced emotional state.

- **Journaling:** Writing about your emotions and experiences can provide clarity, release pent-up feelings, and help you explore solutions to emotional challenges.

- **Gratitude Practices:** Focusing on gratitude can shift your attention from negative emotions to positive aspects of your life, increasing feelings of well-being and happiness.

- Forgiveness: **Forgiving yourself and others can release you from the grip of past hurts and resentments, freeing up emotional energy for more positive uses.**

The Benefits of Emotional Alchemy

- Increased Emotional Intelligence: **Through emotional alchemy, you gain a deeper understanding of your emotional landscape and how to navigate it effectively.**
- Improved Mental Health: **Transforming negative emotions can lead to reduced anxiety, depression, and stress.**
- Enhanced Relationships: **By managing your emotions more effectively, you can communicate more clearly, resolve conflicts more constructively, and build stronger, more positive relationships.**
- Personal Growth: **Emotional alchemy encourages you to use your emotional experiences as opportunities for learning and growth, leading to greater self-awareness and fulfillment.**

Emotional Alchemy represents a powerful approach to personal development, offering tools and insights for transforming emotional challenges into stepping stones toward a more abundant and fulfilling life.

Understanding Emotions as Energy

Understanding emotions as energy involves a profound shift in how we perceive and interact with our emotional states. The concept, often encapsulated by the phrase "energy in motion," highlights the dynamic and influential nature of emotions on our overall being. Here's a deeper dive into this perspective:

The Nature of Emotions

At their core, emotions are not just psychological phenomena but energetic expressions that have a tangible impact on our mental, physical, and energetic health. This understanding is rooted in the belief that everything in the universe, including our thoughts and emotions, is made up of energy. Emotions, therefore, are seen as powerful currents that can move through and influence our entire system.

Emotions as Energy in Motion

The phrase "energy in motion" encapsulates the essence of emotions. They are not meant to be static or repressed; they are designed to flow. When we experience emotions, we are essentially in the midst of an energetic movement within our being. This movement can be harmonious and fluid, leading to feelings of well-being and alignment, or it can be disrupted and blocked, leading to discomfort, stress, and even physical illness.

The Impact of Emotions

The energetic nature of emotions means they have the power to influence not just our mental state but our physical health and the quality of our interactions with the world. Positive emotions like joy, love, and gratitude can enhance our energy levels, boost our immune system, and attract positive experiences and relationships. Conversely, negative emotions like anger, fear, and sadness can deplete our energy, weaken our health, and attract more negativity into our lives.

The Importance of Acknowledging and Experiencing Emotions

Given their powerful impact, it becomes crucial to acknowledge and fully experience our emotions. Suppressing or ignoring emotions does not neutralize their energy; instead, it often leads to emotional blockages that can manifest as physical symptoms, mental distress, or life patterns that keep us stuck in negative cycles. By allowing ourselves to feel our emotions fully, we enable this energy to flow and release, which is essential for our emotional and physical health.

Transforming Negative Emotions

Transforming negative emotions into positive forces is a pivotal aspect of emotional wellness and personal growth. This transformation process begins by recognizing the sources of these emotions and employing various techniques to release them healthily.

Recognizing Emotional Triggers

The first step in transforming negative emotions is to identify what triggers them. These triggers can be external events or internal thoughts that evoke strong emotional responses. Often, the roots of these triggers lie in unresolved issues, deep-seated fears, or limiting beliefs that we may hold about ourselves and the world around us. For example, a fear of rejection may stem from past experiences of being rejected, leading to anxiety in social situations.

Understanding these triggers involves introspection and reflection. It requires us to become observers of our own lives, noting when and why negative emotions arise. This awareness is the foundation for transformation, as it allows us to recognize patterns and address the underlying causes of our emotional responses.

Implementing Emotional Transformation

Transforming negative emotions isn't a one-time task but a continuous process of self-awareness and self-care. Implementing these techniques into your daily life requires commitment and practice. It may be helpful to start small, incorporating one or two practices at a time and observing their effects on your emotional state.

Remember, the goal is not to eliminate negative emotions entirely—that's neither possible nor desirable, as all emotions have their place and purpose. Instead, the aim is to manage these emotions in a way that they no longer have a debilitating effect on our lives, allowing us to move forward with greater freedom, resilience, and positivity.

Transforming negative emotions is essential for emotional alchemy, turning what might initially seem like obstacles into opportunities for growth. By recognizing emotional triggers and employing techniques for emotional release, we can navigate through our emotional landscapes with greater ease and grace, leading to a more balanced, fulfilled, and abundant life.

Part II: The Seeds of Desire

Levels Of Consciousness

The concept of levels of consciousness is a foundational aspect of psychological and spiritual frameworks that describe the different layers of awareness an individual can experience. The subconscious mind is a critical component of this model, interacting with other levels of consciousness to influence our thoughts, behaviors, and overall experience of life. Understanding these levels provides insight into the complex nature of the human mind and how different aspects of our awareness work together.

1. Conscious Mind

The conscious mind represents our current awareness. It's the aspect of our mental process that we can think and talk about rationally. This level includes everything we are aware of at any given moment: our present thoughts, feelings, perceptions, and memories. The conscious mind is where we make decisions, think critically, and process information we receive from our surroundings.

2. Subconscious Mind

The subconscious mind operates just below the level of conscious awareness. It acts as a repository for our automatic skills, acquired behaviors, beliefs, and experiences. This level of consciousness is not actively in our focal awareness, but it significantly influences our actions and feelings. It's where our automatic habits, preferences, and non-decision-based actions reside. The subconscious mind stores all our previous life experiences, our belief system, our memories, our skills—everything that we have seen, done, or thought. It also manages our bodily functions, like breathing and heart rate, which occur without conscious thought.

3. Unconscious Mind

The unconscious mind is a deeper level of awareness that is largely inaccessible to conscious thought. Freud conceptualized it as a storehouse of feelings, thoughts, urges, and memories outside of conscious awareness. It's believed that the unconscious mind holds deep-seated impulses, desires, and fears. These are often the roots of our behavior and emotional responses, which we might not consciously recognize or understand.

4. Collective Unconscious

Coined by Carl Jung, the collective unconscious refers to a level of unconsciousness shared among beings of the same species. It houses archetypes and universal symbols that are inherent in all of us. Unlike the personal unconscious, which is shaped by individual experiences, the collective unconscious is not acquired but inherited. It links individuals to their cultural or universal symbols, providing a shared human experience.

5. Superconscious Mind

In some spiritual and psychological models, the superconscious mind is considered the highest level of consciousness. It represents a state of awareness that transcends individual identity and the limitations of the physical world. It's associated with peak experiences, profound intuition, and a sense of oneness with the universe. The superconscious mind is often described as the source of creativity, spiritual insight, and enlightenment.

Interaction Among Levels

The levels of consciousness are not isolated; they interact with each other in complex ways. The conscious mind makes decisions and navigates daily life based on information and influences from both the subconscious and, to a lesser extent, the unconscious mind. In turn, experiences processed by the conscious mind can affect the content and programming of the subconscious. Intuitive insights and creative ideas often emerge from the superconscious mind, filtering down through the subconscious to become accessible to conscious awareness.

Understanding the levels of consciousness highlights the depth and complexity of human awareness. It underscores the importance of exploring not only our conscious thoughts and actions but also the profound influence of the subconscious and unconscious mind. By becoming more aware of these different levels, we can begin to uncover the root causes of our behaviors and thoughts, leading to greater self-awareness and personal growth.

This book will primarily explore three pivotal realms: the unconscious mind, the conscious mind, and the superconscious mind.

Unconscious Thought -
The Hidden Drive

In the realm of manifestation and the journey toward realizing our deepest desires, the role of unconscious thought is both profound and pivotal. Unbeknownst to many, it is the silent undercurrent that shapes the bedrock of our reality. This chapter delves into the hidden world of our unconscious thoughts—those that simmer beneath the surface of our awareness, influencing our actions, reactions, and the very essence of our lives without our explicit knowledge.

The Power of the Unconscious Mind

The Power of the Unconscious Mind delves into the profound influence and potential of our unconscious mind—a hidden realm that dictates much of our behavior, decisions, and the direction of our lives without our conscious awareness. This exploration reveals how the unconscious mind can be both a formidable ally and an obstacle in our quest for fulfillment and success, particularly in the realm of manifestation.

Our unconscious mind is a vast repository of feelings, thoughts, memories, and desires that, although not in the forefront of our conscious mind, play a significant role in our daily lives. These unconscious thoughts can be both a guiding force and a hindrance to our manifestation efforts, depending on their nature and alignment with our conscious objectives.

The Unseen Force

The unconscious mind operates below the level of conscious awareness, yet it governs a significant portion of our daily activities, reactions, and even our communication. It's where automatic processes, such as breathing and heartbeat, as well as deep-seated beliefs, fears, and desires reside. Unlike the conscious mind, which is engaged with active thinking and decision-making, the unconscious mind stores the programming that influences these thoughts and decisions.

Characteristics of the Subconscious Mind

- Influence on Actions and Feelings: The subconscious mind shapes our reactions and behaviors in ways we might not consciously realize. It draws from a reservoir of our past experiences, learned behaviors, and internalized beliefs to influence how we respond to various situations.

- Residence in the Limbic System: The hippocampus, part of the limbic system in the brain, plays a significant role in the functioning of the subconscious mind. It's involved in the formation of memories and the association of emotional contexts to those memories, acting as a storage center for much of what the subconscious mind governs.

- Storage of Personal Identity: The subconscious mind holds the keys to our belief system, self-image, morals, habits, emotions, fears, secrets, and detailed memories. These elements collectively form the foundation of our personal identity and influence how we perceive ourselves and the world.

- Indistinguishability Between Real and Imagined: One of the most fascinating aspects of the subconscious mind is its inability to differentiate between experiences that are real and those that are vividly imagined. This characteristic is why visualization and positive affirmations can be so powerful, as the subconscious mind can accept these imagined scenarios as true, influencing our emotions and physiological responses accordingly.

- Receptivity to Subliminal Messages: The subconscious mind can pick up on and internalize subliminal messages—signals below the threshold of our conscious awareness. This trait underlines the importance of being mindful of the environment we're exposed to, as subtle cues can influence our subconscious programming.

- Creative Problem-Solving: Often, solutions to problems seem to "come out of nowhere" after we've stopped consciously thinking about them. This is the subconscious mind at work, processing and connecting information in the background and then presenting these insights to our conscious mind.

- Dreams: Dreams are a direct expression of the subconscious mind, offering a window into the thoughts, feelings, and desires that we may not be consciously aware of during our waking hours.

- Access to Psychic Abilities: Some theories suggest that psychic abilities, such as intuition or telepathy, are accessed through the subconscious mind. This belief posits that the subconscious can tap into information and connections beyond the scope of our conscious awareness.

Dual Roles in Manifestation

The unconscious mind plays a dual role in the process of manifestation:

- As a Guiding Force: When your unconscious beliefs and desires are aligned with your conscious goals, the power of the unconscious mind serves as a strong guiding force toward achieving those goals. It silently steers your actions, choices, and reactions in ways that support your conscious efforts, making the path to manifestation smoother and more intuitive.

- As a Hindrance: Conversely, when there's a misalignment between your conscious intentions and unconscious programming, the unconscious mind can act as a significant barrier to manifestation. For example, a deep-seated belief in unworthiness or fear of success can sabotage conscious efforts toward achievement and abundance, often in subtle, unnoticed ways.

Harnessing the Power of the Unconscious Mind

Understanding and harnessing the power of your unconscious mind is crucial for effective manifestation. This involves:

- Self-Reflection and Awareness: Cultivating a practice of introspection can help uncover the beliefs and desires buried in the unconscious mind. Techniques like meditation, journaling, and mindfulness exercises can foster a deeper self-awareness, allowing you to identify and understand your unconscious programming.

- Reprogramming: Once you've identified limiting beliefs or negative patterns, various techniques can help reprogram your unconscious mind to support your conscious goals. These include affirmations, visualization, hypnotherapy, and cognitive-behavioral strategies. Reprogramming the unconscious mind aligns it with your conscious objectives, enhancing your ability to manifest desired outcomes.

- Integration and Harmony: The ultimate goal is to create harmony between the conscious and unconscious minds. This integration ensures that your entire being—conscious and unconscious—is working in unison toward your goals. It's a state where your actions are inspired by deep-seated beliefs that support your aspirations, leading to a more effortless and authentic manifestation process.

The power of the unconscious mind is a critical factor in shaping our reality. By bringing our unconscious programming into alignment with our conscious desires, we unlock a potent force that can propel us toward our goals. The journey to understanding and harnessing this power requires patience, persistence, and a willingness to delve deep into the self. However, the rewards—a life of greater fulfillment, success, and manifestation of our deepest desires—are well worth the effort.

"Unearthing Your Hidden Drives"
Reflect on a recent decision you made. Can you identify any unconscious beliefs or thoughts that might have influenced this decision?

Conscious Thought -
Crafting Your Reality

In the journey of manifestation, conscious thought acts as the architect of our reality. It's through this lens of awareness that we shape our perceptions, decisions, and actions. It delves into the transformative power of conscious thought and the critical importance of bridging the gap between our deep-seated, unconscious desires and our active, conscious awareness. By harnessing the clarity and direction of conscious thought, we set a strong foundation for turning our dreams into reality.

Conscious Mind

The conscious mind is our state of active awareness, where we are fully attuned to our surroundings and ourselves. It's the aspect of our mental processing that we can directly access and control, playing a critical role in how we interpret and interact with the world. This level of consciousness is deeply involved in our daily experiences, decision-making, and intentional actions.

Awareness and Responsiveness

Being in a conscious state means being aware of and responsive to one's surroundings. This awareness allows us to perceive, analyze, and react to different situations in real-time. It encompasses everything from noticing the beauty of a sunset to feeling the discomfort of sitting in an awkward position, prompting us to adjust our posture.

Role of the Amygdala

While the conscious mind involves multiple areas of the brain, it's important to clarify that the amygdala, part of the limbic system, plays a crucial role more in processing emotions, especially those related to survival instincts like fear. The conscious processing of information and decision-making involves broader neural networks, including the prefrontal cortex, which is pivotal for higher-order functions such as planning, reasoning, and self-regulation.

The Filter for Thoughts and Influences

The conscious mind acts as a filter for the immense amount of information we encounter daily. It helps us focus on what's necessary, filtering out irrelevant or less critical data. Considering the staggering volume of information our senses collect at any given moment, this filtering process is essential.

Cognitive Functions

Key functions of the conscious mind include thinking, analyzing information, and controlling movements. It's where rational thought occurs, allowing us to plan, make decisions, and solve problems logically. Additionally, our conscious mind directs our voluntary movements, enabling us to perform tasks and interact physically with our environment.

Processing Capacities

The conscious mind processes an immense amount of information from our senses. Estimates suggest that our senses can receive up to several billion bits of information per second, but our conscious awareness focuses on only about 9 bits at any given moment. This selective attention is crucial for not becoming overwhelmed by the sensory input.

Speed of Sensory Processing

The processing speed of sensory information varies depending on the type of sensory input:

- From sight to touch: approximately 0.071 seconds.
- From touch to sight: approximately 0.053 seconds.
- From sight to hearing: approximately 0.16 seconds.
- From hearing to sight: approximately 0.06 seconds.
- From one ear to another: approximately 0.064 seconds.

These processing speeds illustrate the incredible efficiency of our sensory systems and the conscious mind's capacity to interpret and respond to information from our environment quickly.

The conscious mind is a powerful and essential component of our mental architecture, enabling us to navigate the world through rational thought, decision-making, and direct interaction with our surroundings. By understanding its functions and limitations, we can better appreciate the complex interplay between our conscious awareness and the vast, often unseen, processes of our subconscious and unconscious minds.

The Bridge Between Unconscious and Conscious

Our unconscious mind is a reservoir of desires, beliefs, and experiences that profoundly influence our lives, often without our explicit awareness. Bringing these elements into the light of conscious awareness is crucial. It allows us to understand our true motivations, align our goals more closely with our core selves, and eliminate internal conflicts that may hinder our progress.

Techniques for Uncovering Unconscious Desires

- Mindful Reflection: Spend time in quiet reflection or meditation, focusing on your inner self to recognize desires that bubble up from the unconscious.
- Dialogue Writing: Engage in a written dialogue between your conscious and unconscious self, asking questions and allowing your unconscious to answer.
- Dream Interpretation: Keep a dream journal to capture and explore the themes and messages that your unconscious mind communicates through dreams.

Nurturing Positive, Focused Thoughts

The quality and direction of our conscious thoughts have a profound impact on our ability to manifest our desires. Negative or scattered thinking can cloud our vision and sap our energy, while positive, focused thoughts can clarify our intentions and supercharge our manifestation efforts.

Techniques for Cultivating Positive Thoughts

- Affirmations: Regularly practice affirmations that reinforce your self-worth, capabilities, and the reality you wish to create. Make them specific, positive, and in the present tense.
- Visualization: Dedicate time each day to vividly imagine your desired reality. Use all your senses to make the experience as real as possible, reinforcing the connection between thought and manifestation.
- Gratitude Practice: Cultivate a habit of gratitude by daily listing things you're thankful for. This shifts your focus from lack to abundance, attracting more positivity into your life.

The Power of Focused Intention

Manifestation thrives on clarity and intention. Scattergun approaches dilute our energy and focus, while a laser-like concentration on our goals amplifies our ability to attract what we desire.

Techniques for Sharpening Focus

- Goal Setting: Define clear, measurable, and time-bound goals. Break them down into actionable steps to maintain focus and momentum.
- Mind Mapping: Create a visual representation of your goal and the steps needed to achieve it. This can clarify the path ahead and keep your focus sharp.
- Mindful Practices: Engage in practices that enhance concentration and mental discipline, such as meditation, yoga, or tai chi.

Conscious thought is the powerful tool at our disposal for crafting the reality we desire. By bringing our unconscious desires into the light of awareness and nurturing positive, focused thoughts, we can set the stage for effective manifestation. This chapter offers practical techniques and insights to guide you in consciously shaping your life, emphasizing that the power to change your reality lies within the realm of your conscious thought.

Superconscious Thought -
Unveiling Infinite Possibilities

The concept of the Superconscious Mind represents an elevated level of consciousness that transcends the ordinary human experience, connecting individuals to a pearl of universal wisdom and the collective consciousness often referred to as the Universal Mind or God Consciousness. It is a state of being that goes beyond the limits of the personal self, tapping into a vast reservoir of knowledge, creativity, and intuition. The Superconscious Mind is instrumental in the manifestation process, offering a direct link to profound insights and transformative powers.

Characteristics of the Superconscious Mind

- Transcendent Awareness: The Superconscious Mind embodies a level of consciousness that surpasses individual or normal awareness, aligning with the universal or divine.
- Higher Self Connection: It is often equated with the Higher Self, representing the most enlightened, wise,

and pure aspect of an individual. It's from this place that one can access one's true potential and purpose.

- Access Methods: Accessing the Superconscious Mind can be achieved through practices that elevate one's state of consciousness, such as meditation, specific yoga breathing techniques, and hypnosis. These practices help quiet the chatter of the conscious mind and allow for a deeper connection with the superconscious.

- Group or God Consciousness: This level of consciousness encompasses a sense of unity and oneness with all existence, often described as feeling connected to every living being and the divine or universal intelligence.

- Healing Potential: The Superconscious Mind is believed to have significant healing capabilities, offering insights and energies that can lead to profound emotional, physical, and spiritual healing.

- Omniscience: It is all-knowing, with access to universal truths, wisdom, and knowledge beyond the confines of time and space.

- Access to Akashic Records: The Akashic Records, conceived as a compendium of all human events, thoughts, words, emotions, and intent ever to have occurred, are accessible through the Superconscious Mind, providing insight into past, present, and future possibilities.

- Source of Creativity: It is the wellspring of brilliant ideas, music, art, stories, and groundbreaking concepts. Historical figures like Einstein and Nostradamus are believed to have accessed the Superconscious Mind for their revolutionary insights and predictions.

Effects on Manifestation

The Superconscious Mind plays a crucial role in the manifestation process:

- Alignment with Universal Intent: By connecting with the Superconscious Mind, individuals can align their personal desires with the broader intentions of the universe, ensuring that their efforts to manifest are supported by a higher power.

- Intuitive Guidance: The insights gained from this level of consciousness can guide individuals toward actions and decisions that are in harmony with their highest good, facilitating a smoother manifestation process.
- Enhanced Creativity: Access to the unlimited creative potential of the Superconscious Mind can inspire ideas, solutions, and visions that are innovative and aligned with one's true purpose, making the realization of goals more effective and inspired.
- Spiritual Growth: The process of connecting with and utilizing the Superconscious Mind for manifestation encourages profound spiritual development, fostering a deeper sense of purpose, connection, and fulfillment.

In essence, the Superconscious Mind is a powerful ally in the manifestation process, offering access to universal wisdom, healing, and creative inspiration. By learning to access and collaborate with this higher level of consciousness, individuals can enhance their ability to manifest their desires, align with their higher purpose, and experience profound personal and spiritual growth.

"Consciously Shaping Your World"

How have your repetitive thoughts shaped your current reality, and what conscious changes can you make to align them with your desired reality?

Part III: Bridging Thought and Reality

Action -
Echoes of Intent

In the grand tapestry of manifestation, action serves as the crucial thread that weaves together the fabric of thought and desire into the physical reality of attainment. This chapter, "Action - Echoes of Intent," explores the dynamic role of action in bringing our unconscious and conscious thoughts into fruition. Here, we delve into the indispensable nature of action as the bridge between the internal world of aspirations and the external world of tangible results, offering strategies to ensure that every step taken is in harmony with our deepest intentions.

The Bridge Between Thought and Reality

Manifestation is not merely a mental exercise; it requires the physical momentum of action to translate ephemeral thoughts and desires into concrete outcomes. While our unconscious and conscious minds set the stage with powerful intentions and focused thoughts, it is through action that these intentions and thoughts navigate the realm of possibility and manifest into reality. Actions are, in essence, the echoes of our intent, resonating through the universe to materialize our dreams and aspirations.

Aligning Actions with Goals and Desires

The alignment of our actions with our goals and desires is critical. Misaligned actions can lead us astray, diluting our efforts and leading to outcomes that do not reflect our true aspirations. To ensure that our actions are in sync with our goals, we must adopt a mindful and strategic approach to action-taking.

Strategies for Taking Aligned Actions

- Clarity of Intent: **Before taking action, clarify your intentions. Know what you desire to achieve and why. This clarity will guide your actions and keep you aligned with your goals.**

- Incremental Steps: **Break down your goals into manageable actions. Small, incremental steps create momentum and make larger goals more attainable, ensuring that each action contributes to your overarching intention.**

- Mindful Decision-Making: **With every decision, ask yourself if this choice brings you closer to your goals. Be mindful of the implications of your actions and choose paths that resonate with your intentions.**

- Consistency Over Intensity: **Consistent action, even if small, is more effective than sporadic bursts of effort. Build habits that support your goals, ensuring that your daily actions reflect your desires.**

- Adaptability: **Be prepared to adapt your actions as circumstances change. Flexibility allows you to** navigate obstacles and adjust your approach without losing sight of your goals.

- Reflective Practice: Regularly reflect on the outcomes of your actions. Learn from both successes and setbacks to refine your approach and align your actions more closely with your intentions.

Action - Echoes of Intent

The concept of action as the echoes of our intent underscores the vibrational impact of our deeds. Each action sends out ripples into the universe, signaling our commitment to our goals and attracting the circumstances necessary for their realization. The universe responds to our active participation in the manifestation process, facilitating the alignment of opportunities, resources, and encounters that propel us toward our desired outcomes.

Action is the vital pathway to manifestation, bridging the gap between the world of thoughts and the reality of achievement. Through deliberate, aligned actions, we not only affirm our intentions to the universe but also to ourselves, reinforcing our belief in our ability to manifest our desires.

"Action - Echoes of Intent" serves as a reminder that while the journey of manifestation begins in the mind, it is through our actions that we truly bring our dreams to life.

In the context of manifestation and achieving goals, action encompasses a broad range of activities that translate intention into reality. It's not limited to significant, conspicuous moves but includes a variety of subtler yet impactful steps. Here's how actions can manifest across different activities and involve the five senses to effectively create change:

Examples of Actions

1. Writing Something Down: The act of writing your goals, intentions, or plans serves as a powerful action step. It makes your desires concrete, shifting them from the ephemeral realm of thought into the tangible world. Writing engages the sense of touch (through the physical act of writing) and sight (seeing your words on paper), solidifying your commitment.

2. Telling a Friend: Verbalizing your goals to someone else not only uses the sense of hearing but also strengthens your accountability. Speaking your

intentions out loud brings them into the shared reality, further bridging the gap between the internal and external worlds.

3. Speaking the Thought Out Loud: Similar to telling a friend, speaking your intentions aloud, even to yourself, is a form of auditory affirmation. It leverages the power of sound to reinforce your commitment to your goals, engaging both the sense of hearing and, through the vibration of your voice, the sense of touch.

4. Doing Something: Any physical action taken toward your goal, whether it's researching, networking, or creating something, directly translates thought into physical reality. These actions often engage multiple senses simultaneously, providing a multisensory commitment to your intention.

5. Visualizing Your Goal: Visualization is a potent form of mental action. By vividly imagining achieving your goal, you engage sight (even if only in the mind's eye), sometimes touch, taste, smell, or hearing, depending on what you are visualizing. This process can significantly influence your subconscious and conscious motivations.

Involvement of the Five Senses in Creating Action

Sight: Visual cues often inspire action. Seeing something related to your goal can spark motivation or remind you of your intentions. Visualizing your success engages the brain in a way that mirrors actual achievement, encouraging tangible steps toward your goals.

Hearing: Listening to motivational speeches, affirmations, or simply the act of hearing yourself declare your intentions can reinforce your commitment and prompt action.

Touch: The tactile process of writing down goals, creating vision boards, or even the physical effort toward your goal engages the sense of touch, grounding your intentions in the physical world.

Taste and Smell: These senses might seem less directly related to action, but they can be involved in creating a conducive environment for taking steps toward your goal. For example, the taste of a healthy meal can be part of actions toward health goals, or the smell of incense during meditation can support spiritual aspirations.

Intuition: Beyond the five physical senses, action is deeply connected to our intuitive sense—the inner knowing or gut feeling that guides us toward or away from certain decisions. Listening to and acting on intuition is a key aspect of effectively manifesting our desires.

Action encompasses _any step_, big or small, physical or mental, that moves you closer to your goal. By engaging the senses, these actions become more vivid and impactful, embedding your intentions deeper into your conscious and subconscious mind, and accelerating the manifestation process.

"Reflecting on Your Path to Action"
Think of a goal you recently achieved. What actions did you take that were pivotal in making this goal a reality?

Manifestation -
The Divine Response

In the transformative journey of manifestation, the convergence of thought, emotion, and action into the tangible realization of our desires marks the pinnacle of our efforts. This chapter delves into the heart of the manifestation process, exploring how the interplay of our internal and external worlds shapes the reality we experience. Through a series of inspiring stories and insights, "Manifestation - Seeing Your Desires Come to Life" aims to illuminate the path to turning dreams into reality, offering guidance and inspiration to readers on their manifestation journey.

The Essence of Manifestation

Manifestation is the art of bringing into physical reality the desires and dreams that originate in the mind and heart. It is not a passive process but an *active co-creation* with the universe, requiring clarity of intention, emotional alignment, and consistent action. This chapter explores the key principles that underlie successful manifestation, including the Law of

Attraction, the power of visualization, and the importance of gratitude and positive thinking.

Stories of Successful Manifestation

To illustrate the principles of manifestation in action, this chapter shares stories of individuals who have successfully brought their desires to life. These stories span various aspects of human endeavor, from personal growth and health to career achievements and creative pursuits.

A Health Transformation:

The Journey of Maya: A Health Transformation Story

Maya's journey began on a day much like any other, except for the fact that she found herself sitting in yet another doctor's office, surrounded by the sterile scent of antiseptic and the faint hum of medical machinery. Diagnosed with a chronic health condition that had gradually taken over her life, Maya felt trapped in an endless cycle of treatments, medications, and despair. Her condition, though not life-threatening, severely impacted her quality of life, leaving her exhausted, in constant discomfort, and, most of all, hopeless.

But it was during one of these routine visits that Maya stumbled upon a book in the waiting room, a book that talked about the power of the mind in healing the body. Skeptical but intrigued, Maya began to explore the concept of manifestation and the mind-body connection. She learned about individuals who had overcome significant health challenges through focused intention, positive lifestyle changes, and a steadfast belief in their ability to heal. Inspired by these stories, Maya decided to embark on her own journey of health transformation.

The Power of Focused Intention

Maya started by visualizing her health as she desired it to be, free from pain and full of vitality. Every morning and night, she dedicated time to meditate, focusing her mind on a vivid image of herself healthy, energetic, and thriving. This practice of focused intention became the bedrock of her journey, setting the direction for her thoughts and actions.

Positive Lifestyle Changes

Understanding that manifestation works hand in hand with action, Maya began implementing positive lifestyle changes.

She revamped her diet, opting for whole, nutrient-rich foods that supported her body's natural healing processes. Physical activity, tailored to her condition, became a regular part of her routine, gradually improving her strength and endurance. She also sought out holistic therapies that complemented her medical treatments, such as acupuncture and yoga, which helped reduce her symptoms and improve her overall well-being.

The Power of Belief

Perhaps the most challenging aspect of Maya's journey was cultivating and maintaining a strong belief in her ability to overcome her condition. Despite setbacks and days when her symptoms seemed insurmountable, Maya persisted. She surrounded herself with supportive friends and family, joined online communities of individuals on similar paths, and filled her living space with affirmations and reminders of her healing journey.

The Mind-Body Connection

As weeks turned into months, Maya began to notice significant improvements in her health. Her symptoms, once a constant presence, had started to fade, leaving her with more good days than bad. She felt energized, hopeful, and, most importantly, in control of her health for the first time in years.

The Transformation

A year after beginning her journey, Maya's condition had improved dramatically. Medical tests confirmed what she already knew: her body was healing. While she understood that her condition might require ongoing management, the transformation in her health was undeniable. More than just the physical improvements, Maya had undergone a profound personal transformation. She had discovered the incredible power of her mind to influence her body and, in doing so, had unlocked a new level of wellness and vitality.

Maya's story is a testament to the potential of focused intention, positive lifestyle changes, and the power of belief in manifesting health transformation. It highlights the profound connection between our minds and bodies and serves as an inspiring reminder of our innate ability to influence our health and well-being.

Story: Career Breakthrough

The Ascent of Alex: Manifesting a Career Breakthrough

Alex's story begins in the confines of a cramped, dimly lit office space, where the buzz of fluorescent lights and the clack of keyboards set the rhythm of his daily grind. Working in a job that felt misaligned with his passions and potential, Alex often found himself gazing out the window, dreaming of a career that not only fulfilled him but also ignited his creativity and ambition. He yearned for a breakthrough, a chance to pivot his career toward his true calling—graphic design.

Despite his current role being far removed from the creative industry, Alex held a deep, unwavering belief in his ability to transform his career. He knew that for his dream to materialize, he needed more than just hope; he needed a plan infused with intention and action.

Aligning Actions with Goals

Alex began by defining his goal with precision: to become a graphic designer at a leading creative agency. Understanding the power of aligning actions with intentions, he enrolled in evening classes to hone his design skills and dedicated weekends to building a compelling portfolio. Each step, though small, was a brick in the foundation of his future career.

The Power of Visualization

Having read about the efficacy of visualization techniques in manifesting desires, Alex incorporated this practice into his daily routine. Every morning, before the sun rose, he visualized himself working in his dream job—designing, creating, and collaborating with a team of talented individuals. He imagined the satisfaction of seeing his designs come to life, the vibrant energy of the creative studio, and the sense of pride in doing work that resonated with his soul. This vivid mental imagery fueled his determination, making his dream feel tangible, achievable.

Maintaining an Unwavering Belief

In the face of setbacks and rejections, Alex's belief in his ability to succeed never wavered. He understood that each no brought him closer to a yes. With every portfolio submission and job interview, he refined his approach, gathered feedback, and persisted with a positive outlook. His belief in himself acted as a magnet, attracting opportunities and people that supported his journey.

The Breakthrough

The turning point came unexpectedly on a Tuesday afternoon with a phone call that would change the course of Alex's career. A creative agency, impressed by his portfolio and the determination evident in his application, offered him a position as a graphic designer. The dream that had once seemed distant was now his reality.

Alex's first day at the agency was everything he had visualized and more. Surrounded by creative minds in an environment that celebrated innovation and artistry, he felt a profound sense of belonging and purpose. His journey to this moment— a testament to the power of aligning actions with goals, using visualization as a tool for manifestation, and never losing faith in one's abilities—was a powerful reminder that dreams can indeed become reality.

Alex's career breakthrough story serves as an inspiring example of how focused intention, aligned action, and the power of belief can manifest our deepest desires. It underscores the potential within each of us to reshape our lives and achieve our goals, no matter how distant they may seem. Through persistence, vision, and faith, the path to our dreams is always within reach.

Story: Creative Realization

Elena's Canvas: A Tale of Creative Realization

Elena's story unfolds in the cluttered corner of an old attic that served as her makeshift studio. Surrounded by canvases, paintbrushes, and the faint scent of acrylics, she found solace in her art, a world away from the noise. Despite her undeniable talent, Elena's dream project—a series of large-scale murals depicting the interconnectivity of humans and nature—remained just that, a dream. It was a vision that consumed her thoughts, a project she believed could inspire change and awaken a collective appreciation for the environment. Yet, the path to bringing this vision to life was fraught with obstacles, from financial constraints to finding a platform big enough to house her ambition.

Envisioning the Outcome

Elena knew that for her project to materialize, she needed to see it in her mind's eye with unwavering clarity. She spent countless hours imagining every detail of the murals, from the vibrant hues of the painted landscapes to the emotions they would evoke in viewers. This vivid visualization process became her beacon, guiding her actions and decisions. It was a constant reminder of what she was working toward, infusing her with the motivation to push forward.

Inspired Actions

Understanding that her dream required more than just talent and vision, Elena embarked on a journey to turn her dream into reality. She started small, showcasing her work at local galleries and community spaces, gradually building a name for herself. She applied for grants, reached out to environmental organizations for support, and networked tirelessly with potential sponsors. Each step was taken with intention, rooted in the desire to see her vision come to life.

Elena's path was not smooth. There were moments of doubt, rejection, and frustration that threatened to derail her efforts. Financial hurdles seemed insurmountable at times, and the right opportunities felt just out of reach. Yet, Elena's resilience in the face of these challenges was remarkable. She adapted her strategies, sought creative solutions, and never allowed setbacks to diminish her spirit. Her art became not just a means of expression but a testament to her perseverance.

The Fruition

The breakthrough came when Elena was invited to participate in an international art and environment festival. It was the platform she had been dreaming of—a chance to showcase her vision on a global stage. With the support of the festival organizers and sponsors she had connected with along her journey, Elena's mural series became a reality. The sprawling canvases, rich with color and life, captivated audiences, sparking conversations and drawing attention to the delicate relationship between humanity and the natural world.

The Ripple Effect

The success of Elena's project went beyond the murals themselves. It opened doors to further commissions, collaborations, and speaking engagements, allowing her to spread her message even wider. More than that, it inspired a community of artists and activists to view their work as a catalyst for change. Elena had not only realized her creative vision but had also become a beacon of inspiration for others.

Elena's journey from dreaming in her attic studio to realizing her visionary project is a testament to the power of consistent visualization, inspired action, and resilience. It illustrates that the path to creative realization is paved with challenges but that these obstacles can be navigated with creativity and determination. Elena's story is a reminder to all aspiring artists and visionaries that bringing your dreams to life is possible, one brushstroke at a time.

Guiding Principles for Manifestation

The art of manifestation is not just about wishing for something to happen; it's about creating a conducive environment for those wishes to take root and flourish. Drawing inspiration from the transformative journeys shared, this section outlines core principles and actionable strategies to guide you in applying the power of manifestation in your own life.

Clarity of Vision

The foundation of any successful manifestation begins with a crystal-clear vision of what you wish to achieve. This clarity acts as a beacon, guiding your thoughts, emotions, and actions toward your desired outcome.

- Visualization Techniques: Engage in regular visualization exercises. Picture your goal as vividly as possible, engaging all your senses. Imagine the outcome and the steps leading to it, imbuing each with positive emotion and intention.

- Vision Boards: **Create a vision board that represents your goal. Use images, quotes, and symbols that resonate with your vision to reinforce your intentions every day.**

Emotional Resonance

The emotional energy you align with your vision significantly impacts your manifestation process. Positive emotions can act as a powerful magnet, drawing your desires closer.

- Fostering Positive Emotions: **Integrate practices into your daily routine that enhance feelings of joy, love, and gratitude. This could be as simple as keeping a gratitude journal, engaging in acts of kindness, or dedicating time to activities that bring you joy.**
- Emotional Alignment: **Before taking any action toward your goal, check in with your emotions. Ensure that your actions are not just driven by logic but are also imbued with positive emotional energy.**

Aligned Action

Manifestation requires more than just positive thinking; it _demands_ action that is in direct alignment with your goals. These actions bridge the gap between the intangible and the tangible.

- Action Steps: **Break down your goal into actionable steps. Make each step realistic and achievable, ensuring that it directly contributes to your larger vision.**
- Overcoming Obstacles: **Recognize that obstacles are part of the journey. Approach each with a problem-solving mindset, asking yourself how it can be turned into an opportunity for growth or a different approach.**

Surrender and Trust

Perhaps one of the most challenging aspects of manifestation is finding the balance between effort and surrender—knowing when to push forward and when to let go and trust the process.

- Trust in the Universe: Cultivate a deep trust in the universe or whatever higher power you believe in. Remind yourself that you are supported and that what is meant for you will not pass you by.
- The Art of Letting Go: Learn to let go of the need to control every outcome. Surrender involves faith in the timing and wisdom of the universe, understanding that sometimes, what we manifest may arrive in forms different from what we initially envisioned.

The principles of manifestation—clarity of vision, emotional resonance, aligned action, and surrender and trust—serve as a roadmap to turning your dreams into reality. By incorporating these principles into your daily life, you engage in a co-creative process with the universe, opening doors to endless possibilities. Remember, manifestation is a journey of becoming as much as it is about achieving. Embrace each step with intention, openness, and gratitude, and watch as the world unfolds in alignment with your deepest desires.

Key Elements of Successful Manifestation

- Clarity of Intention: Successful manifestation begins with a clear and specific intention. Knowing precisely what you want to achieve is crucial because it sets the direction for your thoughts and actions. Clarity helps you focus your energy and avoid the dispersion of your efforts on conflicting desires.

- Emotional Alignment: Your emotional state plays a significant role in the manifestation process. Emotions are powerful vibrational energies that can attract corresponding experiences. Feeling as though your desire has already been fulfilled and aligning your emotions with the joy, gratitude, or satisfaction that achieving your goal would bring amplifies your ability to manifest.

- Consistent Action: While manifestation involves working with the energetic and metaphysical aspects of reality, it also requires practical, consistent action in the physical world. These actions should be aligned with your goals and propelled by your intention and emotional energy.

- Belief and Trust: **Believing in the possibility of your desired outcome and trusting in the process are fundamental to successful manifestation. Doubts and skepticism can introduce resistance and hinder the flow of energy needed to bring your desires into reality.**

- Openness and Receptivity: **Being open and receptive to the ways in which your desires can manifest is important. Sometimes, opportunities come in unexpected forms. Staying attuned to possibilities and being flexible in your approach can lead to successful outcomes.**

Measuring Success in Manifestation

Measuring success in manifestation extends beyond the simple metric of whether or not a specific desire or goal was achieved. It encompasses a broader spectrum of personal development and enlightenment that accompanies the journey toward realizing one's aspirations. This multifaceted approach to gauging success encourages a deeper appreciation of the transformative process inherent in manifestation.

The Realization of Desired Outcomes

At its core, the success of a manifestation can indeed be observed in the physical realization of a set goal or desire. Whether it's acquiring a new job, healing a relationship, improving health, or achieving financial stability, the tangible attainment of these objectives signifies a direct correlation between intent and outcome. This realization serves as a powerful affirmation of the individual's ability to co-create with the universe, reinforcing confidence in the manifestation process.

The Value of Personal Growth and Insights

Beyond the tangible outcomes, the journey of manifestation offers invaluable opportunities for personal growth and self-discovery. This aspect of success is often overlooked but is equally, if not more, significant.

- Self-Awareness: The process of manifestation encourages a deep introspection, prompting individuals to examine their true desires, motivations, and the limiting beliefs that may hinder their progress.

This heightened self-awareness fosters a more profound understanding of one's inner workings and potential for growth.

- Resilience and Adaptability: Manifestation challenges individuals to navigate setbacks and obstacles with resilience and creativity. The ability to adapt and persevere in the face of adversity is a testament to personal growth, cultivating qualities of strength and flexibility that extend beyond the realm of manifestation.

- Emotional Intelligence: Aligning thoughts, emotions, and actions with one's desires requires a nuanced understanding of one's emotional landscape. The manifestation journey enhances emotional intelligence, teaching individuals to navigate their feelings with greater awareness and intention.

- Expanded Consciousness: The practice of manifestation often leads to a broader perspective on life and a deeper connection with the universe. This expanded consciousness opens the individual to new possibilities, ways of thinking, and a greater sense of interconnectedness with all that is.

The Holistic Measure of Success

Thus, while the achievement of specific goals is a clear marker of success in manifestation, the journey itself offers a wealth of experiences and lessons that contribute to an individual's overall well-being and evolution. The true measure of success encompasses both the external achievements and the internal transformations experienced along the way.

Success in manifestation, therefore, can be seen as a holistic integration of achieving one's desires while simultaneously experiencing personal growth, emotional development, and an expanded awareness. This comprehensive approach ensures that regardless of the immediate outcomes, every step taken in the manifestation process contributes to the individual's journey toward a more fulfilled and self-aware existence.

The Continuous Journey of Manifestation

Manifestation is not simply a destination to be reached but a continuous process of collaboration with the universe. This chapter underscores the importance of recognizing manifestation as a fluid and ongoing journey, emphasizing the journey's inherent value as much as the outcomes it produces. Readers are encouraged to welcome the growth and insights gained from their experiences, stay receptive to new opportunities, and find joy in each step taken toward the fulfillment of their aspirations.

The essence of successful manifestation lies in the transformation of one's intentions and desires into tangible reality, marking the realization of one's initial vision. This transformative journey extends beyond mere wishful thinking, requiring a harmonious alignment of thoughts, feelings, and actions toward one's objectives. This process is deeply intertwined with the principle that the universe acts as a receptive field of energy, engaging with our own energy projected through our convictions, thoughts, and behaviors.

Manifestation unfolds as a perpetual journey of creation alongside the universe, inviting individuals to appreciate the unfolding path, remain adaptable to unfolding opportunities, and celebrate the progress made toward achieving their dreams. This perspective shifts the focus from solely achieving specific goals to valuing the personal evolution and broader understanding that comes from engaging in the manifestation process.

The Journey Beyond the Outcome

Achieving success in manifestation is equally about the journey undertaken as it is about reaching the final goal. This process serves as a powerful avenue for honing your ability to actively shape your own reality. It's a discovery of the profound impact your thoughts and emotions wield, the critical role of purposeful action, and the profound significance of embracing trust and acceptance. The journey's unexpected shifts and turns play a crucial part in deepening your grasp of manifestation's core principles fostering personal growth along the way.

Manifestation transcends the mere achievement of a particular outcome, embedding itself in the significant learnings and personal development that occurs as you take an active role in molding your reality. This path sheds light on how your innermost thoughts and feelings drive your life's direction, emphasizes the need for intentional actions, and imparts the vital lessons of trusting the process and learning to release control. The twists and challenges encountered enrich your mastery of manifesting, marking milestones in your personal journey toward self-discovery.

At its heart, successful manifestation is the fruition of your initial vision, brought to life through a harmonious dance of desire, belief, emotional vibrancy, and decisive action. It affirms your capacity to work in tandem with the universe, transcending mere goal achievement to spark a journey of self-realization and empowerment. Manifestation is fundamentally about translating your deepest aspirations into reality by leveraging a concerted mix of intention, faith, emotional alignment, and action. This process not only materializes your desires but also heralds a period of profound self-growth and empowerment, inviting you on a transformative expedition of discovering and reshaping your essence.

"Manifestation - Seeing Your Desires Come to Life" serves as both a beacon of hope and a practical toolkit for those on the path to realizing their dreams. By intertwining the core tenets of manifestation with real-life triumphs and hands-on strategies, this chapter seeks to ignite the spark of potential within each reader. It encourages an active engagement with the process of manifestation, guiding you to translate your innermost aspirations from the ethereal planes of thought and feeling into the palpable reality of your everyday life. Armed with the insights and techniques shared herein, you are equipped to embark on a journey of transformation, one where you hold the power to mold your existence and witness the unfolding of your dreams into your waking reality. Let this chapter be your map and compass as you navigate the expansive seas of possibility, steering toward the shores of your most cherished goals.

"Celebrating Your Manifestation Milestones"
Recall a time when something you desired manifested in your life. How did it feel, and how closely did the outcome match your initial intention?

Part IV: Nurturing the Spiritual Bond

Emotional Response -
The Feedback Loop

Emotional Response - The Feedback Loop" explores the spectrum of emotions accompanying the manifestation process, focusing on how our feelings toward our successes and setbacks can inform and refine our path forward. Emotions are not just reactions but signals, pointing us toward deeper insights and opportunities for growth in pursuing our desires.

The concept of the feedback loop in manifestation is akin to a mirror reflecting our internal states and desires through the outcomes we experience. This loop is fundamentally about observing and evaluating the results of our manifestation efforts and using our emotional reactions to these outcomes as a compass for future actions. Whether we find joy and satisfaction or disappointment and dissatisfaction in what we manifest serves as a crucial determinant in guiding our next steps. This process ensures that our journey of manifestation is dynamic, responsive, and continually aligned with our truest desires.

Evaluating Outcomes

When we manifest something into our lives, our emotional response to the outcome provides immediate feedback. Positive emotions, such as joy, gratitude, and fulfillment, indicate alignment with our core desires and intentions. They confirm that what we've brought into our reality resonates with our inner selves, motivating us to pursue similar paths of manifestation in the future.

Conversely, if the outcome elicits negative emotions like regret, disappointment, or a sense of misalignment, it serves as a critical cue. This feedback suggests that the manifested outcome may not truly align with our deeper desires or that our approach to manifestation needs recalibration.

Decision-Making and Future Manifestations

The feedback loop influences our decision-making process regarding whether to maintain what we've manifested or to adjust our sights and efforts toward different goals. If we cherish the outcome and it enriches our lives, we're likely to seek to manifest similar experiences or outcomes again. This positive reinforcement strengthens our manifestation techniques and beliefs, enhancing our confidence in our ability to co-create with the universe.

If the outcome isn't what we hoped for or doesn't bring the satisfaction we anticipated, this feedback is invaluable. It prompts introspection and reassessment of our desires, intentions, and methods. This reflective process is essential for growth and learning, helping us to refine our approach to manifestation. We learn to pivot, to let go of what doesn't serve us, and to realign our actions and intentions with our true desires.

The Continuous Cycle of Manifestation

The feedback loop in manifestation underscores the importance of being in tune with our emotional responses and using them as guidance. It highlights manifestation as a continuous cycle of desire, action, outcome, and reflection. By paying attention to how we feel about our manifested outcomes, we become more adept at navigating the path toward fulfilling our deepest desires. This ongoing cycle encourages us to remain active participants in the co-creation of our reality, constantly learning from our experiences and refining our approach to align more closely with our envisioned life.

The 5 Steps to Manifestation

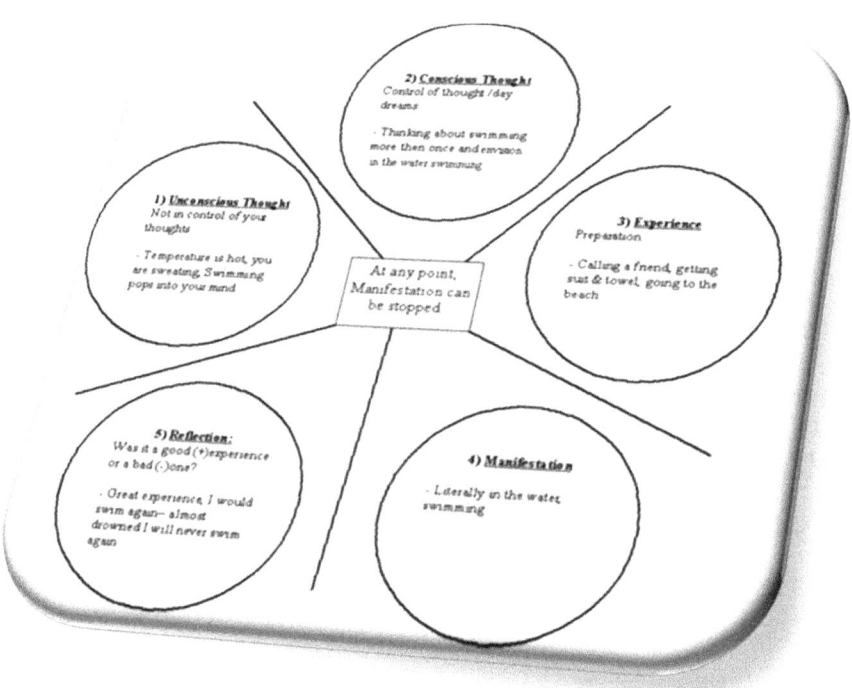

1. Unconscious Thought

2. Conscious Thought

3. Action

4. Manifestation

5. Emotional Reflection +/-

These five steps form a holistic framework for understanding the journey from the seed of thought to the fruit of manifestation, underscored by continuous reflection and adaptation based on our emotional responses to the outcomes of our efforts.

The Five Steps to Manifestation: A Story of a Day at the Beach

Step 1: Unconscious Thought – A Spark Ignites

On a sweltering summer's day, while laboring away in the garden, Jack felt the sun's intense heat beating down on him. For a fleeting moment, as sweat beaded on his forehead, the thought of swimming in cool water flickered through his mind. It was an unconscious whisper, a subtle invitation from the universe, gone as quickly as it came, buried under the day's immediate demands.

Step 2: Conscious Thought – A Desire Takes Shape

As the day wore on and the heat intensified, the thought returned. This time it lingered, evolving into a conscious dream of diving into the refreshing embrace of the sea. Jack envisioned himself swimming alongside his good friend Lisa, laughing and splashing away the afternoon heat.

With the vision solidifying in his mind, Jack didn't hesitate. He phoned Lisa, who eagerly agreed to the spontaneous plan. They could both use the escape. Jack wrapped up his work, gathered his swim gear, and, with a sense of expectation, picked up Lisa for their beach getaway.

Step 4: Manifestation – The Vision Becomes Reality

Before long, Jack and Lisa found themselves at the beach, the ocean stretching out before them. They waded in, and with each stroke, Jack's vision of swimming was realized. The water was as rejuvenating as he had imagined, and for a glorious hour, his desire for relief from the heat was fulfilled in every splash.

As the sun began to set, they retreated from the water. On the drive back, Jack reflected on the day's events. He felt grateful for the reprieve the ocean had provided and was already looking forward to future swims. Lisa, however, seemed quieter than usual. Later, she confessed that the experience had been overwhelming for her, as she wasn't as strong a swimmer as she had thought. While Jack's emotional response was one of contentment and anticipation for more aquatic escapades, Lisa's experience led her to a different realization.

This contrast in their emotional responses to the same event was significant. Jack's positive emotions reaffirmed his love for swimming and a signal to keep pursuing this activity, which brought him joy and relief. For Lisa, her initial excitement had given way to introspection. She understood that she had confronted a personal limit, and it left her with a mix of respect for the ocean's majesty and a desire to better prepare for future challenges.

Jack's emotions completed a feedback loop that would encourage the manifestation of more swimming in his future. His response was clear: the joy of swimming was a desire that resonated deeply with him, something to be nurtured and repeated.

Lisa's emotional feedback, while more complex, was just as valuable. It would shape her future intentions differently. Perhaps she would take swimming lessons, or maybe she would find other ways to enjoy the water that felt safer to her. Or, she might decide to engage with nature in a different context altogether, one where she felt more in her element.

After manifesting their shared goal, their divergent emotional responses highlighted a profound lesson: manifestation is a deeply personal journey where emotional reflection is crucial in shaping future intentions. As they drove home under the twilight sky's orange hues, Jack and Lisa understood that their journey of manifestation was not just about achieving an outcome but also about learning from their responses to it, using these insights to guide their next steps in the dance with the universe.

Unconscious Thought:

This level involves the thoughts and desires that reside beneath our conscious awareness, influencing our behavior and reactions without us fully realizing it. It's the bedrock of our deepest beliefs, fears, and motivations that shape our reality from the shadows.

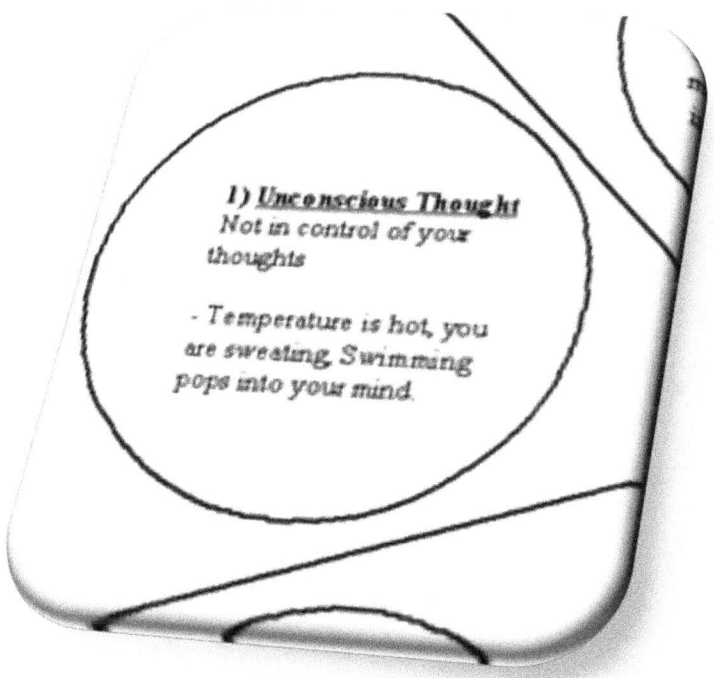

1) **Unconscious Thought**
Not in control of your thoughts

- Temperature is hot, you are sweating. Swimming pops into your mind.

Conscious Thought:

Represents the thoughts and decisions we're actively aware of and engage with. Conscious thought is where intentionality lives, allowing us to direct our focus, make decisions, and set goals based on our desires and aspirations.

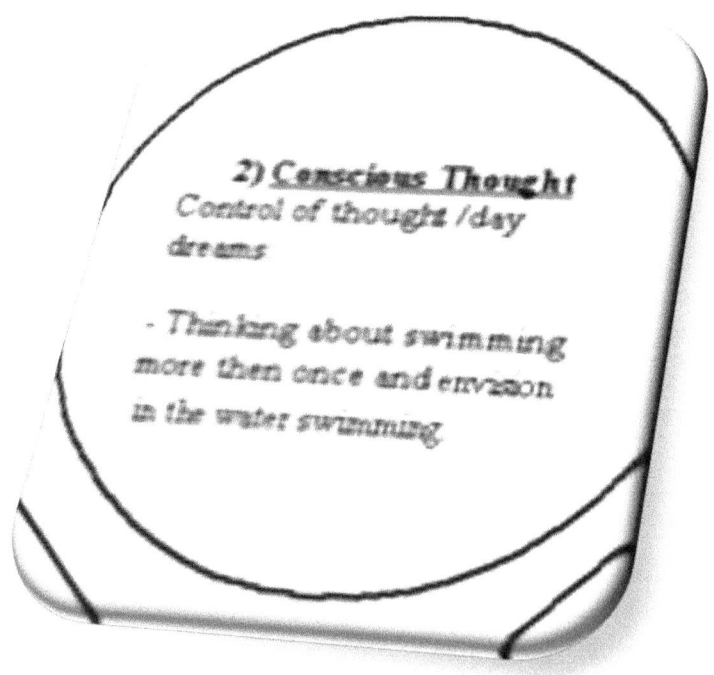

Action:

The tangible steps we take to bring our thoughts and desires into reality. Action bridges the gap between the internal world of thought and the external world of results. It encompasses all deliberate moves, big or small, geared toward achieving our set intentions.

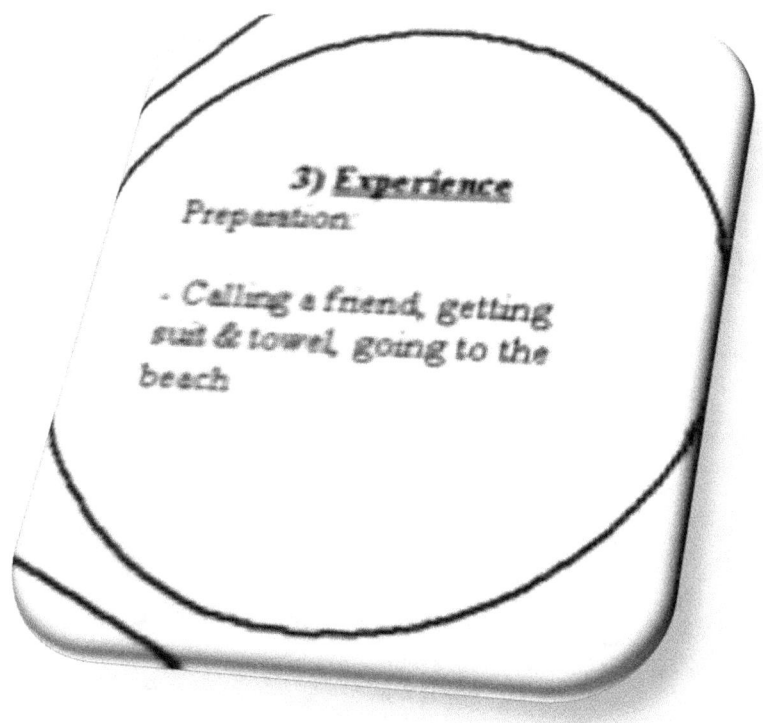

3) **Experience**
Preparation:

- Calling a friend, getting suit & towel, going to the beach

Manifestation:

The process of turning intentions and desires into tangible outcomes. It's the culmination of unconscious and conscious thoughts, fueled by emotion and action, resulting in the realization of our goals and dreams in the physical world.

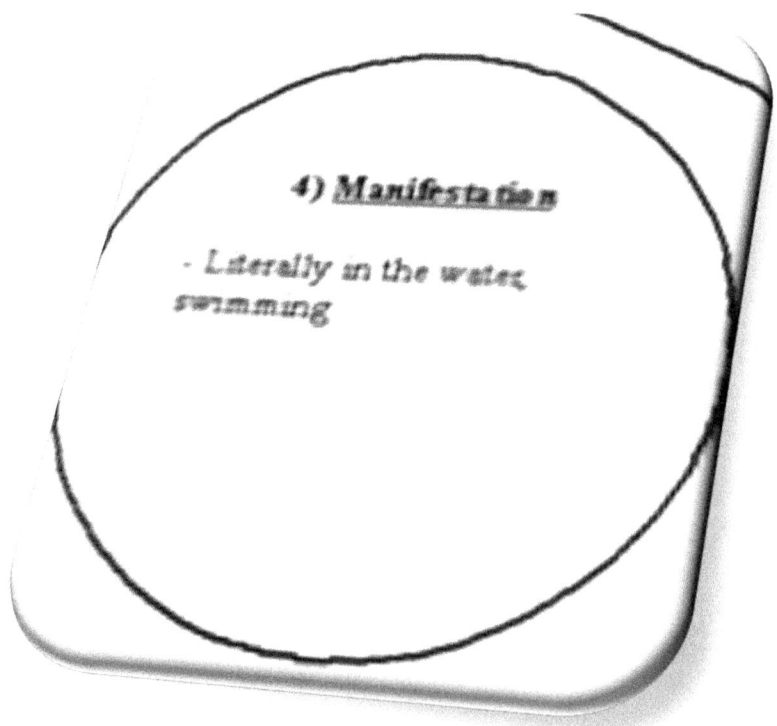

4) Manifestation

- Literally in the water, swimming

Emotional Reflection (+/-):

The feedback mechanism is where we assess our emotional responses to the outcomes of our manifestation efforts. Positive emotions indicate alignment and satisfaction with the results, encouraging similar endeavors in the future. Negative emotions signal a misalignment, prompting reassessment and adjustment of our intentions, thoughts, or actions for future manifestations.

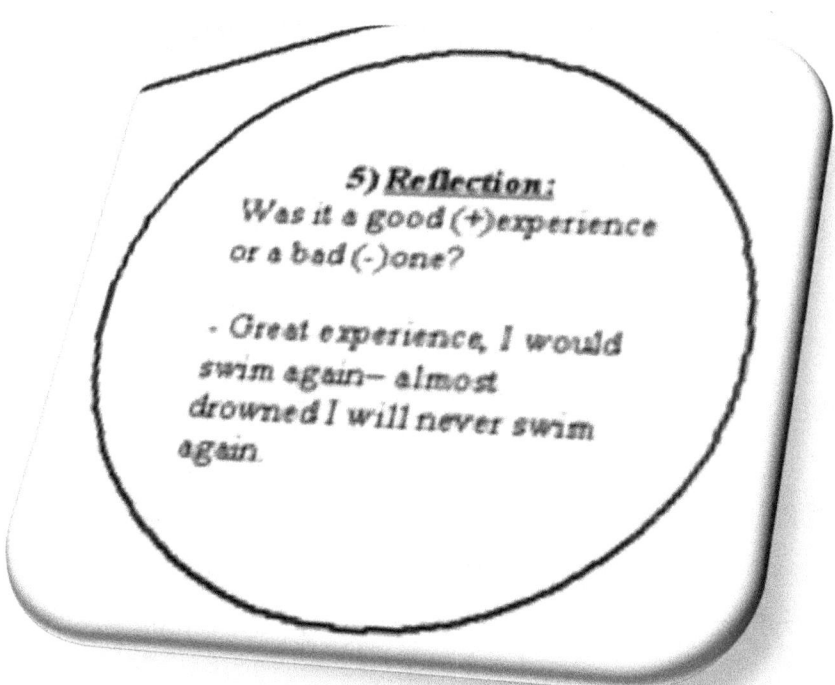

5) Reflection:
Was it a good (+)experience or a bad (-)one?

- Great experience, I would swim again— almost drowned I will never swim again.

Emotional Response -
The Vibrational Harmony

In the nuanced journey of manifestation, emotional responses play a critical role, acting as a compass that guides our path toward achieving our dreams. This section, "Emotional Response - The Vibrational Harmony," delves into the spectrum of emotions accompanying the manifestation process, from the delight of successes to the discouragement of setbacks. It underscores the importance of understanding and harnessing these emotional responses, not mere reactions but vital feedback that can inform and refine our journey.

Navigating Emotional Responses to Manifestation

The path to realizing our desires is inherently emotional. Each step, whether forward or backward, elicits a range of feelings that reflect our deep-seated hopes, fears, and aspirations.

- Celebrating Success: The joy and satisfaction derived from witnessing the fruition of our efforts are profound. Success reinforces our belief in the manifestation process and in our own co-creative power. It's a testament to our alignment with our intentions and the vibrational harmony we've achieved with the universe.

- Learning from Setbacks: Conversely, setbacks can evoke feelings of disappointment, frustration, or doubt. However, these emotions are not indicators of failure but are, instead, invaluable feedback. They signal areas where our alignment might have faltered, offering clues for recalibration.

Emotions as a Guide for Refinement

Our emotional responses serve as a dynamic guide in the manifestation journey, offering insights that can help further refine our desires and actions.

- Reflective Awareness: By reflecting on our emotional responses, we can gain clarity on what truly resonates with us and what doesn't. This awareness allows us to fine-tune our intentions, ensuring they are in true alignment with our core desires.

- Actionable Feedback: Emotions highlight the effectiveness of our actions and strategies. Positive emotions encourage us to continue down our chosen path, while negative emotions prompt us to reassess and adjust our approach.

Cultivating Emotional Resilience and Flexibility

Embracing the full range of emotional experiences is key to maintaining vibrational harmony in the face of both triumphs and trials.

- Emotional Resilience: Cultivating resilience enables us to navigate the highs and lows with grace, viewing each experience as a stepping stone toward greater understanding and fulfillment.
- Flexibility in Emotional Responses: Learning to fluidly adapt our emotional responses ensures that we remain open to the lessons and opportunities presented by each phase of the manifestation process.

Nurturing the Spiritual Bond

The emotional journey of manifestation is deeply intertwined with our spiritual growth. As we traverse the highs and lows, we're invited to deepen our connection with the universe, recognizing that each emotional response is a dialogue with the divine. This chapter emphasizes the spiritual dimension of our emotional experiences, guiding readers to nurture this bond, thereby enriching their manifestation journey with a sense of purpose, connectedness, and divine harmony.

"Emotional Response - The Vibrational Harmony" explores the pivotal role emotions play in the manifestation process. By understanding and navigating our emotional landscape with awareness, resilience, and flexibility, we harness the power of our feelings to serve as a guide, propelling us toward our desired outcomes. This chapter encourages readers to embrace their emotional responses as crucial feedback, refining their desires and actions in a continuous loop of vibrational alignment and spiritual growth.

"Navigating Your Emotional Landscapes"

After achieving a desired outcome, what emotional response did you experience, and how did it inform your next steps or adjustments in your manifestation process?

Part V: Deepening Your Divine Connection

Beyond Requests - Building a Relationship

In the grand dance of existence, forming a bond with the universe or a higher power transcends mere appeals for personal gain. This chapter, "Beyond Requests - Building a Relationship," explores the essence of cultivating a profound connection with the cosmos, a relationship that is as nurturing as it is enriching. Here, we delve into the means and modalities through which one can develop a rapport with the universal energies, anchoring oneself in a spiritual communion that informs and transforms every aspect of being.

Connecting with the Universe

The universe is not a distant, impersonal expanse; rather, it is a vibrant, conscious matrix that responds to our intentions and actions. Establishing a connection with the universe is akin to entering a dialogue where both parties listen and respond. It's a relationship built on trust, openness, and a willingness to engage with the larger forces at play.

Wallace Wattles

Wallace Wattles is the author who laid much of the groundwork for modern understandings of the Law of Attraction with his book "The Science of Getting Rich," which was published in 1910. In this book, Wattles discusses various principles related to wealth and success, including the concept of a "Thinking Substance" from which all things are made. This substance fills the interspaces of the universe, and it is through our interaction with it via our thoughts that we are able to form the reality around us, including attracting wealth. Wattles's ideas on the formless substance and the power of thought significantly influenced the New Thought Movement and many subsequent authors, including those behind "The Secret."

The concept of the "Thinking Substance" is central to Wallace Wattles's philosophy in "The Science of Getting Rich." It is a metaphysical idea that suggests a formless substance or universal intelligence is present throughout the universe and is the source of all material things. Here's a deeper look into Wattles's concept:

The Nature of Thinking Substance

- Omnipresent: Wattles posits that this Thinking Substance is everywhere at all times. It fills the interspaces of the universe, functioning as a raw material from which all things are created.
- Responsive to Thought: According to Wattles, this substance is responsive to human thought in a way that it can be shaped or impressed upon to create physical reality. He suggests that thoughts and beliefs can influence this substance to bring about circumstances and opportunities in the material world.

- Formless and Intelligent: The Thinking Substance is formless, meaning it is not visible or tangible, yet it possesses intelligence. It is not just matter, but it is smart matter that can understand and act upon our desires.

- Creative Power: Wattles attributes the creation of the universe to this substance, suggesting that it holds creative power. This power can be harnessed by individuals through their thoughts to create their reality.

Human Interaction with Thinking Substance

- Positive Thinking: Wattles encourages the practice of positive thinking and visualization as methods to communicate desires to the Thinking Substance. By maintaining a clear and positive mental picture of what one desires and acting in ways that align with that vision, an individual can cause the Thinking Substance to bring about those desires.

- Gratitude: Gratitude plays a key role in Wattles's philosophy. He believes that being grateful for what one already has puts the individual in harmony with the Thinking Substance, and this alignment helps attract more wealth and success.

- Purposeful Action: While Wattles emphasizes the importance of thought, he also insists that thought must be accompanied by purposeful action. He asserts that action is critical and that individuals must act in certain ways – in the "Certain Way," as he refers to it – to effectively manifest wealth.

The Influence of Thinking Substance

Wattles's concept of the Thinking Substance has had a profound influence on the New Thought movement and, later on, the Law of Attraction as presented in works like "The Secret." It provides a framework for understanding how individuals might align their thoughts to a larger universal force to manifest their desires. While modern interpretations may vary, the essence of Wattles's idea continues to resonate with many people seeking to understand the connection between their internal thought processes and external experiences in life.

The Space Between Computer Bits and Bytes

The space between computer bits and bytes in the context of quantum computing involves a fundamental and profound shift from classical computation models to those based on the principles of quantum mechanics. In classical computing, data is processed in bits, which exist in a state of either 0 or 1. However, in quantum computing, the basic unit of data is the quantum bit, or qubit, which can exist simultaneously in states of 0, 1, or any quantum superposition of these states.

Quantum Superposition and Entanglement

The concept of quantum superposition allows a qubit to occupy multiple states at once, which means that a quantum computer can process a vast amount of possibilities simultaneously. This is drastically different from classical bits, which can only be in one state at any given time.

Entanglement is another quantum phenomenon where qubits become intertwined in such a way that the state of one (no matter the distance) can depend on the state of another. This linkage can potentially lead to extremely fast processing speeds and the ability to solve complex problems much more efficiently than classical computers.

The Quantum Void

The space between these quantum bits and bytes can be thought of as the "quantum void." It's not empty space in the traditional sense but a field of potential where the phenomena of superposition and entanglement reside. In this realm, the limitations of classical physics are transcended, opening up a landscape where information behaves in fundamentally novel ways.

Quantum Computing and Information

Quantum computing leverages these unique properties to perform certain types of calculations much more efficiently than classical computers. Problems that involve searching through large data sets, optimizing complex systems, or simulating the behavior of molecules and materials can potentially benefit from quantum computing's ability to operate within this quantum void.

The exploration and manipulation of data in the quantum space between bits and bytes herald a new era of computing with implications for cryptography, material science, pharmaceuticals, and beyond. As research and technology advance, our understanding and capability to harness the power of the quantum realm continue to expand, promising to unlock new possibilities in processing power and information theory.

The Space Within a Breath

The space within a breath, particularly during the hold, can be a profound experience, as you've discovered. In yogic practice, this is referred to as "kumbhaka," and it is an essential aspect of pranayama or breath control exercises. The hold after an exhale is called "bahya kumbhaka," and after an inhale, it's known as "antara kumbhaka."

The Vastness of the Hold

During the hold, whether after inhaling or exhaling, there is often a palpable stillness, a pause in the constant flow of life where time seems to expand. This stillness is not just a physical cessation of movement but can also be a mental and spiritual suspension of the usual chatter and distraction. For some, this space can feel infinite and immeasurable, a moment of potential and depth that is both part of the self and beyond it.

The Experience of Timelessness

In these moments of kumbhaka, practitioners sometimes report experiences of timelessness or vastness, as if they've touched upon something eternal. It can be a mesmerizing state where the usual boundaries of self and time dissolve. Some describe it as tapping into a universal rhythm or the very essence of being.

The Body's Homeostasis

Physiologically, during the breath hold, the body experiences a temporary state of homeostasis. This can have a concentrating effect on the mind. However, if prolonged, especially in the case of beginners or those not trained in breathwork, it can trigger an involuntary response to resume breathing as the body's survival mechanisms kick in to restore oxygen levels and remove carbon dioxide.

Advanced yogis and Tibetan monks, through years of disciplined practice, learn to enter and sustain these states of kumbhaka, along with deep meditative states, for extended periods. They have trained their bodies and minds to minimize the metabolic processes, allowing them to go for days without food or water, although these are exceptional practices and should not be attempted without proper guidance and preparation.

Meditation and breathwork are profound practices that leverage the often-overlooked spaces within the breath to cultivate mindfulness, emotional balance, and mental clarity.

Meditation and the Space Within the Breath

Meditation often involves focusing on the breath as it flows in and out of the body. Within this practice lies a special moment—a pause, a space between the inhalation and exhalation. This gap, although brief, is a powerful place of potential where practitioners can experience a deep sense of stillness and presence. It's in these interludes that many report feeling a connection to something greater than themselves, a boundless space of awareness that extends beyond the physical confines of the body.

Techniques Involving the Breath's Space

- Mindful Breathing: Paying close attention to the natural rhythm of your breath, noticing the slight pauses between each cycle.
- Box Breathing: A structured method where you inhale, hold, exhale, and hold again, all for equal counts, creating a box pattern that includes space within and between breaths.
- Breath Awareness: Simply observing the breath without alteration, bringing awareness to the spaces within each breath, and observing the thoughts and emotions that arise.

Breathwork and the Expansion of Consciousness

Breathwork uses a variety of breathing techniques to influence a person's mental, emotional, and physical state. Conscious manipulation of the breath can lead to altered states of consciousness, providing new perspectives on internal psychological landscapes. The controlled use of breath creates a bridge to the less tangible aspects of our being and can result in profound personal transformations.

- Stress Reduction: Rapid or rhythmic breathing techniques can reduce stress by shifting the body's balance from the sympathetic (fight or flight) to the parasympathetic (rest and digest) nervous system.
- Emotional Release: Certain breathwork methods can evoke emotional responses and facilitate the release of suppressed feelings, creating space for healing.
- Spiritual Connection: Sustained breath practices can induce trance-like states, offering experiences of transcendence and oneness with the universe.

In many spiritual traditions, breath is seen as the vital bridge connecting the physical to the spiritual, signifying the flow of life force itself. This life force is known by many names across different cultures: 'prana' in Indian philosophy, 'chi' in Chinese medicine, and 'ruach' in Hebrew texts, among others. It is commonly believed that by controlling and observing the breath, one can influence one's physical, emotional, and energetic states, thereby promoting a deeper connection with the spiritual realm.

The Spiritual Practices of Breath

- Mindful Breathing: Mindfulness practices often start with breath awareness—simply observing the natural rhythm of inhalation and exhalation. This awareness brings about a sense of presence and centeredness, allowing practitioners to anchor themselves in the present moment, often leading to a state of heightened clarity and calmness.
- Pranayama: In yogic practices, pranayama, which literally means 'control of the life force,' involves a series of breathing exercises designed to master the breath and, by extension, the energy or 'prana' within the body. This mastery is said to awaken dormant energies, cleanse the body's energy channels, and balance the energetic centers known as chakras.
- Qi Gong and Tai Chi: These Chinese practices combine movement, meditation, and breath control to maintain health and increase vitality. The breath is used to guide

qi (energy) through the body, promoting healing and spiritual development.

- Sufi Breathing: Sufi traditions use breathwork as a means to reach states of ecstasy and divine union. Breathing exercises in these traditions are often combined with the chanting of sacred names or phrases, deepening the meditative state.

The Metaphysical Aspect of Breath

In religious texts, breath is often associated with the soul or spirit. The act of God breathing life into the first human in the creation stories suggests an intimate link between the divine spark and the breath of life. In spiritual terms, controlling and directing one's breath is akin to aligning with the rhythms of the cosmos, harmonizing individual consciousness with universal consciousness.

Breath as a Healing Tool

The therapeutic aspects of breath are also recognized in various spiritual doctrines. Controlled breathing can lead to the release of emotional blockages, promote relaxation, and facilitate healing both in the physical and metaphysical sense.

Breathing techniques are employed in many healing modalities, with the understanding that breath is the most direct means of influencing the autonomic nervous system.

Breath in Meditation and Contemplation

In meditation, breath serves as a focal point for the mind, a tool to transcend the chatter of the ego and enter deeper states of consciousness. It is both a physical and spiritual act; by concentrating on the breath, mediators can journey into the depths of their being and experience a sense of oneness with all that is.

The spiritual dimension of breath is a profound testament to its significance beyond mere biological function. It is an expression of the interconnectedness of life, a rhythmic echo of the universal pulse, and a doorway to inner realms and higher states of awareness. Through the breath, we touch the essence of existence and find a path to the vastness within.

The connection between breath, bits and bytes, and the "Thinking Substance" may not be immediately apparent, given that they belong to seemingly disparate realms: spirituality, technology, and metaphysical philosophy, respectively.

However, upon closer examination, we can find a unifying thread rooted in the concept of foundational elements that inform existence, communication, and creation in their respective domains.

Breath: The Essence of Life and Spiritual Connectivity

In spiritual traditions, breath is the essential life force, a fundamental component that sustains life and acts as a bridge between the material and spiritual worlds. It represents the invisible yet palpable force that animates and energizes, an element both within us and part of the greater whole.

Bits and Bytes: The Building Blocks of Digital Communication

In computing, bits and bytes are the fundamental elements of digital communication and processing. They form the basis of information in the digital realm, allowing for the creation, storage, and exchange of knowledge. Although they are the smallest units of data in computing, their combinations and permutations create complex systems and virtual environments, echoing the multiplicity of the universe from simple origins.

Thinking Substance: The Metaphysical Matrix of Manifestation

Wallace Wattles's "Thinking Substance" is the primordial essence from which all physical forms are manifested according to thoughts and beliefs. It suggests a universal canvas responsive to human consciousness, similar to the responsiveness of a computer program to its coded instructions.

The Interconnectedness of Spaces

These three concepts—breath, bits and bytes, and the Thinking Substance—although operating on different planes of understanding, all symbolize the fundamental resources through which systems operate and interact:

Breath symbolizes the flow and connectivity of life and spirit.

Bits and bytes represent the binary foundation through which all digital forms are created and communicated.

Thinking Substance symbolizes the malleable potential from which reality itself is shaped by thought.

In essence, each one of these spaces can be seen as a canvas or conduit for transformation and manifestation within their spheres. Breath transforms energy and intention into life and spiritual experience. Bits and bytes transform digital signals into information and virtual experience. Thinking Substance transforms human thought into physical experience.

Moreover, they all imply a certain level of interaction and responsiveness—a feedback loop where an input (be it breath, digital command, or thought) leads to an output (life force activation, computational process, or physical manifestation). They represent a layer of fundamental components that react and reshape themselves to create a desired outcome, highlighting a universal pattern of creation and interconnectivity that transcends individual domains.

Space

The concept of "space" — whether we interpret it as the metaphysical space between thoughts and reality, the digital space between bits and bytes, or the spiritual space influenced by breath — intriguingly connects with the five steps to manifestation (Unconscious Thought, Conscious Thought,

Action, Manifestation, Emotional Response). Each of these steps navigates through different "spaces" to transform desires into reality, illustrating an intricate dance between the intangible and the tangible.

Unconscious Thought: The Seed in the Void

In the realm of manifestation, unconscious thoughts exist in the deep, unseen spaces of our mind, akin to seeds buried in fertile soil. This space, while not immediately visible, is rich with potential. It's where our deepest desires and fears reside, subtly influencing our conscious choices and actions, much like the unseen forces of the universe that shape the cosmos.

Conscious Thought: Shaping the Ether

As we bring unconscious thoughts into the realm of conscious thought, we begin to shape the "space" around us with intention. This phase involves actively engaging with the formless potential, similar to an artist visualizing a sculpture in a block of marble. The "space" here is the canvas of imagination, where possibilities are endless, and our focused thoughts begin to give form to desires.

Action: Bridging Spaces

Action represents the physical movement through space, turning the ethereal into the material. It's the bridge between the inner world of thought and the outer world of manifestation. Just as a sculptor chisels away at marble, our actions in physical space carve out the reality we wish to see. This step is where the digital "bits and bytes" transform ideas into tangible outcomes, embodying the transition from potential to actuality.

Manifestation: The Emergence in Physical Space

Manifestation is the culmination of thoughts and actions materializing in physical space. It's the point where the seed of an unconscious thought, shaped by conscious intent and nurtured by action, blooms into reality. This space is no longer formless or virtual but tangible and experiential, a concrete expression of our desires and intentions brought to life.

Emotional Response: The Feedback Loop through Inner Space

The emotional response to manifestation navigates the inner space of our being, closing the loop of the manifestation process. It's a reflective phase where the internal landscape is influenced by the external outcome. This space is deeply personal and introspective, offering insights and lessons that fuel future cycles of manifestation. Our reactions—joy, gratitude, disappointment—act as signals, guiding the refinement of our desires and the reshaping of our intentions.

In essence, the "space" in its various forms plays a crucial role in each step of the manifestation process, serving as the medium through which thoughts are transformed into reality. It's a dynamic and interactive field, constantly influenced by our intentions, actions, and responses, highlighting the interconnectedness of all things in the journey of bringing our desires to fruition.

Practices for Establishing Connection

- Meditation: Meditation serves as a gateway to communion with the universal consciousness. It allows us to quiet the mind and attune our spirit to the subtler frequencies of existence. Through meditation, we can experience the oneness that permeates all things, fostering a sense of interconnectedness with the universe.

- Gratitude: Cultivating a habit of gratitude opens our hearts and aligns our energy with the frequency of abundance. By acknowledging and appreciating the blessings we receive, we enter into a positive flow of energy, inviting more of what we are thankful for into our lives.

- Asking for Signs: Sometimes, we seek confirmation of our connection with the divine. Asking for signs can be a way to receive guidance or reassurance. This act is a humble acknowledgment of the universe's wisdom and a readiness to heed its cues.

- Nature Immersion: Spending time in nature, observing the intricate beauty and balance of the natural world, can deepen our connection to the universe. Nature is a tangible expression of the divine, and by immersing ourselves in it, we sync our rhythm with the universal pulse.

- Service to Others: Engaging in acts of kindness and service shifts our focus from self-centered goals to the well-being of others, expanding our hearts and aligning us with the high vibrational frequency of compassion and generosity. When we serve others without expectation, we open channels of abundance and purpose, which can reflect back into our own lives in unexpected ways. Serving others can be an expression of our highest intentions, reinforcing the interconnectedness of all beings and affirming that by uplifting those around us, we contribute to a collective manifestation of positivity and growth.

Signs and Synchronicities - **Understanding Divine Communication**

Signs and synchronicities are often interpreted as meaningful coincidences or alignments that occur in our lives, which many believe to be forms of divine communication. These experiences transcend ordinary explanations and are perceived to carry messages, guidance, or affirmations from the universe, the divine, or our higher selves. Recognizing and understanding signs and synchronicities can deepen our spiritual journey, providing insights and directions that align with our soul's path.

Nature of Signs and Synchronicities

- Signs: Typically, a sign is a specific symbol, occurrence, or event that appears in one's life and holds personal or universal significance. Signs might come in the form of numbers, animals, words, or events that resonate with the individual on a deep level, often answering a call or a question posed by the person, either consciously or unconsciously.

- Synchronicities: Coined by Carl Jung, synchronicities refer to the meaningful coincidences that occur in one's life that seem too significant to be merely chance. These can be sequences of events that align perfectly to guide, affirm, or redirect a person's path, suggesting an underlying pattern or purpose orchestrated by a higher intelligence or the interconnected web of existence.

Understanding Divine Communication

- Personal Relevance: The key to understanding signs and synchronicities often lies in their personal relevance to the individual experiencing them. They might answer a question, affirm a decision, or provide comfort during times of uncertainty. The personal connection to the sign or synchronicity is what imbues it with meaning and significance.
- Patterns and Repetition: Frequently, signs and synchronicities are recognized through patterns or repetition—seeing the same numbers repeatedly, encountering the same animal or word multiple times,

or experiencing a series of events that point toward a specific direction or answer.

- Emotional Resonance: A strong emotional reaction or a sense of awe, peace, or wonder often accompanies the recognition of a sign or synchronicity. This emotional resonance is a key aspect of divine communication, signaling the significance of the message being received.

Interpreting and Acting on Divine Communication

- Reflection and Meditation: Taking time to reflect on the sign or synchronicity, perhaps through meditation or journaling, can help in deciphering the message or guidance it holds. Intuitive insights often arise during quiet moments of contemplation.
- Alignment with Intuition and Values: When interpreting signs and synchronicities, ensuring that the perceived message aligns with one's intuition and core values is essential. Divine communication should feel empowering and in harmony with one's truth.

- Openness and Receptivity: Maintaining an open and receptive state allows for a greater flow of divine communication. Being attached to a specific outcome or message can sometimes block the awareness of signs and synchronicities that are present.

Prayer Is Asking, Meditation Is Listening

The phrase "Prayer is asking, meditation is listening" encapsulates two fundamental aspects of many spiritual practices, highlighting the complementary nature of prayer and meditation in the pursuit of spiritual growth, understanding, and connection.

Prayer: The Act of Asking

Prayer is a deliberate act of communication with the divine, a higher power, or the universe, depending on one's beliefs. It is often characterized by the articulation of thoughts, wishes, desires, or seeking guidance and assistance. Prayer can be seen as an outward expression of one's hopes, fears, gratitude, and reflections directed toward something greater than oneself. It embodies the active, yang aspect of spiritual practice—expressive, projective, and sometimes petitionary in nature.

- Expressing Desires and Needs: In prayer, individuals vocalize their innermost desires, hopes for assistance in their troubles, or clarity for their doubts, effectively "asking" the universe or the divine for what they seek.
- Gratitude and Acknowledgment: Prayer also serves as a vehicle for expressing gratitude, recognizing the blessings in one's life, and acknowledging the presence and role of the divine or the universe in everyday existence.

Meditation: The Art of Listening

Meditation, in contrast, is often described as a receptive practice where the focus is on stillness, observation, and opening oneself to the subtleties of experience and inner wisdom. It is about creating a space of silence and calm within which one can listen—to the self, to the divine, or to the universe. Meditation embodies the passive, yin aspect of spiritual practice—receptive, reflective, and inward-looking.

- Receiving Guidance and Insights: **Through meditation, individuals create an openness to receive insights, guidance, or simply a greater sense of peace and clarity from the universe or their higher self. It's in the silence and stillness that one can "hear" or perceive the subtle messages or truths that often go unnoticed in the hustle of daily life.**

- Connecting with Inner Self and the Universe: **Meditation facilitates a deep connection with the inner self and, by extension, the universal consciousness. This practice allows for a profound listening that transcends words, touching the essence of being and the interconnectedness of all.**

The Complementary Nature of Prayer and Meditation

Together, prayer and meditation form a complete cycle of spiritual dialogue—asking and listening, speaking and being silent, expressing and receiving. This dynamic interplay enhances spiritual awareness and growth, offering a holistic approach to understanding and relating to the divine or the universal consciousness.

- A Complete Spiritual Communication: **Just as in any meaningful relationship, communication involves both speaking and listening. Prayer and meditation together ensure that this spiritual communication is balanced and full.**

- Cyclical Growth and Understanding: **By engaging in both practices, individuals can find a deeper sense of balance and harmony in their spiritual journey. Prayer allows for the expression of the soul's desires and concerns, while meditation offers a quiet space for the answers, guidance, or peace to emerge.**

In essence, understanding the roles of prayer and meditation as asking and listening, respectively, enriches the spiritual journey, offering paths to deeper understanding, connection, and harmony with the universe and oneself.

Spiritual Connection and the 5 Steps to Manifestation

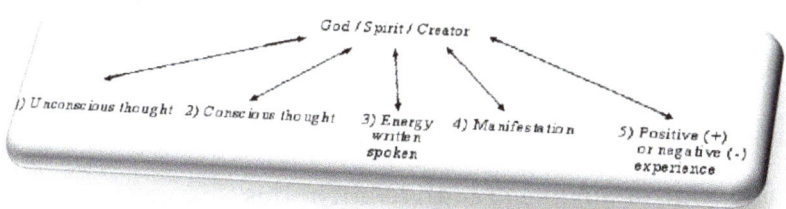

The journey from an unconscious thought to the realization of a desire and the subsequent emotional reflection is a complex interplay between the individual and the universe or spirit. This process can be broken down into five key stages, each of which represents a different level of interaction and response from the spiritual realm.

1) Unconscious Thought

At this initial stage, thoughts flutter through our minds like leaves in the wind—countless, constant, and without deliberate intention. These are the background noise of our psyche, often unnoticed and fleeting. The spirit or the universe observes this ceaseless stream of unconscious thoughts but does not engage with them directly. Without focused intention, these thoughts are like seeds falling on barren land, unlikely to take root.

2) Conscious Thought

When a thought becomes conscious, it stands out from the mental chatter. It is pondered upon and rolled over in the mind with intention and consideration. This shift catches the attention of the spirit. The thought is no longer just a whisper in the wind but a call into the void, signaling a potential for something more. At this juncture, the universe begins to listen more intently, recognizing the deliberate energy being funneled into a specific direction or desire.

3) Action (Energy)

Energy is the commitment behind the thought, the action that breathes life into desire. It might manifest as speaking about the intention, researching, planning, or any action that moves the thought from the realm of the mind into a tangible effort. This is where the spirit perceives the seriousness of the individual's intent. The universe not only listens but starts to respond, aligning forces to support the burgeoning manifestation. It's the acknowledgment from the universe that the individual is ready to co-create their reality.

4) Manifestation

Manifestation is the culmination of this process, the birthing of thought into physical reality. It is the universe's response to the call of conscious thought and directed energy. At this stage, what is asked for—and believed to be deserved—begins to materialize. This underscores the importance of clarity and purity in one's desires, as the universe provides precisely what is sought, for better or worse. It is advised to frame desires within the context of one's higher good, ensuring that what is manifested aligns with the truest path of the individual's soul.

5) Positive or Negative Emotional Reflection

The final stage is the emotional response to the manifested reality. This reflection acts as a feedback loop to the universe. Positive experiences reinforce the manifestation cycle, encouraging the individual and the universe to continue this co-creative journey. Conversely, negative experiences or reflections serve as lessons, highlighting misalignments between desire and true need or revealing underlying beliefs that may sabotage one's ability to manifest. This step determines whether the cycle begins anew, refined by the insights and emotional responses derived from the previous manifestation.

This process is a dynamic dialogue between the individual and the universe, a dance of desire, intention, and realization. Each step, from the seed of an unconscious thought to the reflection upon the manifested outcome, is an opportunity for growth, understanding, and deeper alignment with one's highest good and the universal flow.

The Journey to Mexico: A Tale of Manifestation

Chapter 1: A Fleeting Dream

On a mundane Tuesday afternoon, amidst the hum of his office, Alex found his mind wandering to the sandy beaches of Mexico—a fleeting daydream of sunshine and waves that vanished as quickly as it came. Unbeknownst to him, this brief longing was a whisper into the universe, barely noticed amid the cacophony of unconscious desires echoing through the cosmos.

Chapter 2: A Seed of Intention

Weeks later, during a casual catch-up, Alex's friend, Marco, mentioned his upcoming trip to Mexico and extended an invitation. That night, alone with his thoughts, the idea took root. The universe, attuned to the shift from idle dream to deliberate contemplation, began to lean in, sensing the germination of true intent.

Chapter 3: Stirring the Energies

Driven by a burgeoning excitement, Alex took concrete steps. He visited a travel agency, gathering brochures that painted vivid pictures of azure waters and golden sunsets. Conversations with friends moved from hypothetical musings to definitive plans, and soon, a deposit anchored his commitment. The universe watched, recognizing the earnest energy Alex invested, feeling the palpable shift from mere thought to determined action.

Chapter 4: The Manifestation

The day arrived when Alex, passport in hand, found himself stepping onto Mexican soil, the warm air embracing him like an old friend. It was a moment of realization—his daydream, once as ephemeral as a cloud, had condensed into the tangible joy of the experience. The universe, in its vast orchestration, had aligned to his desires, mirroring back the essence of his ask.

Chapter 5: The Reflection

Mexico was everything Alex had imagined and more. Yet, as he explored its landscapes and cultures, he encountered both the enchantment and the challenges of his dream destination. Each experience was a thread in the tapestry of his journey, weaving together moments of bliss with strands of discomfort.

As the trip concluded, Alex found himself at a crossroads of emotion. The joy of fulfilling his wish battled with the realization that the idealized Mexico of his dreams was, like all places, a complex reality. This emotional feedback loop became a crucible for growth, prompting introspection on the nature of his desires and the authenticity of his aspirations.

The universe observed, ready to respond to Alex's evolving journey. For while the trip to Mexico was a manifestation realized, the deeper journey—the exploration of desire, the understanding of self, and the recognition of true fulfillment—was just beginning.

As Alex returned, he carried with him not just memories but a newfound wisdom. His experiences in Mexico—both luminous and lacking—served as a beacon for future manifestations. Armed with a clearer understanding of his wishes and their motivations, Alex stepped forward, ready to dream anew, with the universe as his silent partner, ever-responsive to the call of genuine intent.

In this dance of desire and discovery, Alex learned that manifestation is not merely about acquiring or achieving but about aligning with one's higher good and embracing the journey with all its revelations and realities. And so, with a heart open to both the gifts and the lessons of the universe, Alex ventured forth, his soul attuned to the endless possibilities of co-creation.

Conclusion

Signs and synchronicities serve as gentle nudges, affirmations, or guiding lights on our spiritual journey, offering insights and directions from a higher intelligence or the interconnected fabric of existence. Recognizing and understanding these forms of divine communication can enrich our spiritual practice, providing clarity, comfort, and a sense of being supported and guided on our path. They remind us of the magical, synchronistic nature of the universe and our connectedness to everything within it.

Part VI: Living in Divine Flow

Sustained Co-Creation - **Maintaining Manifestations**

Living in Divine Flow explores the essence of sustained co-creation and the continuous nurturing required to maintain manifestations in alignment with one's highest good and the universal current. This phase of the journey is not merely about achieving singular goals but about integrating the practice of manifestation into the fabric of daily life, ensuring that each moment is lived in harmony with the divine flow. It's about recognizing that manifestation is a continuous process of co-creation with the universe, where the maintenance of achieved desires is as crucial as their initial realization.

Sustained Co-Creation

- Continuous Alignment: Living in divine flow requires a constant alignment of one's thoughts, emotions, and actions with their highest intentions and the universal will. It involves regularly checking in with oneself and the universe to ensure that the path being walked is in harmony with one's soul's purpose.

- Adaptation and Evolution: Desires and goals are not static; they evolve as individuals grow and learn. Sustained co-creation means being open to this evolution, allowing manifestations to adapt and change. This flexibility ensures that what is manifested continues to serve one's highest good, even as that definition changes.

Maintaining Manifestations

- Gratitude as Foundation: Gratitude not only accelerates the manifestation process but is essential in maintaining the blessings already received. Regularly expressing gratitude for one's manifestations keeps the energy around them positive and vibrant, reinforcing their presence and power in one's life.

- Energetic Upkeep: Just as a garden requires watering and weeding, manifestations need energetic upkeep. This can involve clearing negative energies, reinforcing intentions through affirmation and visualization, and remaining vigilant against complacency. It's about keeping the energetic space around one's manifestations clear and charged.

- Integration into Being: True maintenance of manifestations comes from integrating them into one's sense of self and life. When a manifestation becomes a natural part of one's existence, its presence is solidified not just in the physical realm but in the spiritual and emotional realms as well. This integration fosters a deep sense of fulfillment and purpose.

Challenges and Solutions

- Living in divine flow is not without its challenges. Distractions, doubts, and external pressures can divert one from this path. However, the key to overcoming these challenges lies in:

- Regular Practice: Making manifestation practices a regular part of one's routine helps one stay attuned to the divine flow. Meditation, journaling, and nature walks are just a few practices that can keep one connected to their co-creative power.
- Community and Support: Surrounding oneself with a supportive community that understands and respects the path of manifestation can provide encouragement and inspiration during challenging times.
- Learning from Experience: Viewing every outcome as an opportunity for learning and growth transforms potential obstacles into stepping stones, keeping one aligned with the divine flow.

Living in Divine Flow through Sustained Co-Creation and Maintaining Manifestations is about embracing the journey of co-creation as a way of life. It's a commitment to growing with one's manifestations, allowing them to evolve, and integrating them into the very essence of one's being. This part of the journey emphasizes that the art of manifestation is not just about creating what we desire but about living in harmony with those creations, continually nurturing them, and ourselves, in alignment with the universal current of abundance and love.

The Ripple Effect -
Impacting the World

The Ripple Effect - Impacting the World Around You delves into the profound concept that our personal manifestations have the power to extend beyond our individual lives, influencing the broader community and contributing to the collective upliftment of humanity. This section explores the interconnectedness of all things and how, through intentional living and manifestation, individuals can set into motion a cascade of positive change that reverberates throughout the world.

The Nature of the Ripple Effect

Interconnectedness: At the heart of the ripple effect is the understanding that we are all interconnected, part of a vast, intricate web of life. Our thoughts, actions, and energies do not exist in isolation but interact with and impact the energies around us.

Influence of Positive Change: When an individual focuses on manifesting positivity—whether in the form of love, success, health, or harmony—that energy does not remain confined to their personal experience. It radiates outward, affecting the immediate environment and, subsequently, the larger world.

Manifestations as Catalysts for Collective Upliftment

Inspiration and Motivation: Witnessing someone achieve their dreams or live in a state of joy and fulfillment can serve as a powerful source of inspiration and motivation for others. It can spark a belief in the possibility of change and encourage others to embark on their own journey of manifestation.

Shared Benefits: Certain manifestations have inherently collective benefits. For example, manifesting a community garden not only fulfills an individual's desire to connect with nature and cultivate beauty but also creates a shared space for community engagement, education, and environmental sustainability.

Energetic Shifts: On a subtler level, the energy associated with positive manifestations contributes to an overall shift in the collective consciousness. As more individuals manifest from a place of love, peace, and abundance, these qualities become more prevalent in the world's energetic fabric, paving the way for a more harmonious existence.

The Responsibility of Manifestation

Conscious Creation: **Recognizing the ripple effect brings with it a responsibility to manifest consciously, considering not just personal desires but their potential impact on the community and the planet.**

Intention for the Greater Good: **Incorporating intentions for the greater good into personal manifestation practices can amplify the positive ripple effect. Setting intentions that align with the well-being of others and the planet ensures that one's manifestations contribute to a collective upliftment.**

Practical Ways to Leverage the Ripple Effect

Acts of Kindness: **Simple acts of kindness and generosity, inspired by one's own journey of manifestation, can start a ripple effect of positivity and compassion in the community.**

Community Projects: Engaging in or initiating community projects that aim to improve the quality of life for others channels the power of manifestation for collective benefit.

Sharing Knowledge and Experience: Sharing insights, lessons, and successes from one's manifestation journey can empower others, providing tools and encouragement for their paths.

The Ripple Effect - Impacting the World Around You underscores the profound potential of individual manifestations to catalyze positive change on a broader scale. By acknowledging our interconnectedness and embracing the responsibility to manifest with awareness and intention for the collective good, each person has the power to contribute to a wave of transformation that uplifts and enriches the world around us. Through conscious co-creation, we can realize our desires and play a pivotal role in shaping a world that reflects our highest aspirations for love, harmony, and abundance.

"Your Impact on the Tapestry of Life"
Can you think of a personal achievement that had a positive effect on those around you? Describe the impact and how it made you feel.

Part VII: Understanding and Overcoming Manifestation Blockages

The Shadow of Unmanifestation

Understanding and Overcoming Manifestation Blockages delves into the manifestation process's often overlooked but crucial aspect: the shadow of *un*manifestation. This section explores the various blockages and obstacles that can impede our ability to manifest our desires, understand their origins, and provide strategies to overcome them. It shines a light on the darker, hidden elements of our psyche and life experiences that may hold us back from realizing our true potential and living in alignment with our highest aspirations.

The Nature of Manifestation Blockages

- Emotional Barriers: Unresolved emotions, such as fear, doubt, guilt, or unworthiness, can create significant blockages in the manifestation process. These emotions can stem from past traumas, societal conditioning, or personal beliefs and often operate subconsciously, undermining our efforts to manifest.

- Mental Limitations: Limiting beliefs about oneself, the world, or the nature of reality can stifle the manifestation process. These mental barriers, often ingrained through upbringing or cultural messages, shape our perception of what is possible and deserving.

- Energetic Disruptions: Our energetic field can be disrupted by various factors, including toxic relationships, unhealthy environments, or misaligned actions. These disruptions can create disharmony within ourselves and with the universe, obstructing the flow of manifestation.

- Self-Reflection and Awareness: **The first step in overcoming manifestation blockages is to cultivate self-awareness. This involves reflecting on our innermost fears, desires, and beliefs, bringing to light the hidden aspects of our psyche that may be contributing to our blockages.**

- Healing and Release: **Addressing and healing emotional wounds is crucial. This can be achieved through therapy, spiritual practices, or self-help techniques aimed at releasing trapped emotions and transforming limiting beliefs.**

- Aligning with Higher Self: **Reconnecting with our higher self and aligning our actions, thoughts, and emotions with our true essence can help dissolve blockages. This alignment fosters a sense of harmony and coherence, essential for manifesting our desires.**

Strategies to Overcome Manifestation Blockages

- **Mindfulness and Meditation:** Practices that foster mindfulness and meditation can help quiet the mind, allowing us to observe and shift negative patterns. Meditation, in particular, can facilitate a deeper connection with our higher self, providing clarity and insight into overcoming blockages.

- **Affirmations and Visualization:** Utilizing positive affirmations and visualization techniques can reprogram the subconscious mind, replacing limiting beliefs with empowering ones. Visualizing oneself overcoming blockages and manifesting desires can create a powerful mental blueprint for success.

- **Energy Work and Cleansing:** Engaging in energy work, such as Reiki, yoga, or Qigong, can help clear energetic disruptions. Cleansing practices, like smudging with sage or taking salt baths, can also purify one's energetic field, enhancing the flow of manifestation.

Embracing the Journey

Understanding and overcoming manifestation blockages is an integral part of the spiritual journey. It requires patience, persistence, and compassion toward oneself. By embracing the shadow of unmanifestation, we not only clear the path for our desires to materialize but also embark on a profound journey of self-discovery and healing. This process allows us to emerge more connected, empowered, and in tune with the universe, ready to co-create our reality with clarity and purpose.

Identifying Blockages

Identifying blockages in the manifestation process is a crucial step toward realizing your desires and living a life that's aligned with your highest good. These blockages, often rooted in deeper psychological, emotional, or energetic patterns, can subtly undermine your efforts to manifest. By becoming aware of these hindrances, you can begin the work of clearing them, thereby enhancing your ability to attract what you truly desire.

Psychological and Emotional Blockages

- Limiting Beliefs: **Deep-seated beliefs about oneself, others, or the world that restrict one's perception of what's possible. These might include feelings of unworthiness, beliefs that one doesn't deserve happiness or success, or that certain goals are unattainable.**

- Fear and Doubt: **Fear of failure, fear of success, or general uncertainty can paralyze action and cloud intention, acting as a significant barrier to manifestation. Doubts about one's abilities or the** feasibility of one's desires can also inhibit the flow of positive energy.

- Past Traumas: Unresolved traumas from one's past can have a profound impact on the present, shaping one's expectations for the future and often resulting in blockages that prevent the manifestation of one's desires.

Energetic Blockages

- Misaligned Actions: Actions that are not in harmony with one's true desires or higher self can create energetic dissonance, obstructing the manifestation process.
- Toxic Relationships and Environments: Surroundings and relationships that drain energy or create negativity can impede one's vibrational frequency, making it difficult to attract positive outcomes.
- Collective Unconscious: The concept of the collective unconscious, first introduced by Carl Jung, refers to the part of the unconscious mind that is shared among beings of the same species and contains archetypes and universal experiences. In the context of

manifestation and energy, the collective unconscious plays a significant role in how the energies and attitudes of others can influence our own ability to manifest our desires.

Influence of the Collective Unconscious on Manifestation

- Shared Energies and Beliefs: The collective unconscious encompasses shared beliefs, energies, and attitudes that can subtly influence individual thoughts and feelings. When these collective energies align with negativity, fear, or doubt, they can seep into our personal energy fields, potentially clouding our manifestation efforts with these same frequencies.

- Archetypes and Social Roles: Within the collective unconscious lie archetypes and societal expectations that can shape our desires and the way we pursue them. Sometimes, the goals we set for ourselves are more reflective of these collective narratives than our true, individual aspirations, leading us to manifest a path that is not entirely our own.

- Synchronicities and Universal Connections: On a more positive note, the collective unconscious can also facilitate synchronicities—meaningful coincidences that guide us toward our goals. These synchronicities are manifestations of the interconnectedness of all things and can provide signs, help, and opportunities that align with our intentions.

Navigating the Influence of Others' Energies

- Awareness and Discernment: Cultivating an awareness of when and how the collective unconscious—or the energies of those around us—influences our manifestation process is crucial. This awareness allows for discernment, enabling us to separate our true desires from those imposed by collective beliefs or external pressures.
- Protecting and Cleansing Your Energy: Engaging in practices that protect and cleanse your personal energy field can help mitigate the impact of external energies. Techniques such as meditation, visualization of protective barriers, and the use of crystals or sage

are examples of how individuals can shield themselves from unwanted influences.

- Intentional Community Building: Surrounding ourselves with a community that supports our highest goals and vibrational frequency can counteract the negative influences from the collective unconscious. By fostering connections with those who share our values and aspirations, we can amplify positive energies and create a microcosm of support for our manifestation efforts.

Contribution to the Collective: just as the collective unconscious can influence us, we can influence it. By focusing on positivity, healing, and abundance, we contribute these energies back into the collective, potentially uplifting others and creating a more supportive, energetic environment for manifestation universally.

The collective unconscious and the energies of those around us can significantly affect our manifestation process, for better or worse. By becoming mindful of these influences, actively protecting and cleansing our energy, and choosing our communities wisely, we can navigate these waters more effectively. Furthermore, by contributing positive energies back into the collective, we not only facilitate our manifestation journey but also support the collective elevation toward higher consciousness and fulfillment. Understanding and working with the concept of the collective unconscious thus becomes a powerful tool in our manifestation toolkit, enabling us to navigate both personal and shared energies toward the realization of our deepest desires.

Countering The Effects

Countering the effects of others' energy control or overpowerment involves a combination of self-awareness, boundary-setting, energy protection techniques, and personal empowerment strategies. When you're aware of being influenced or drained by the energies of others, taking proactive steps can help you maintain your equilibrium and personal power. Here are strategies to help you counter these effects:

1. Strengthen Self-Awareness

- **Recognize Influence:** Learn to recognize when your energy or mood is being affected by others. This could manifest as feeling drained, anxious, or upset after interactions.
- **Identify Patterns:** Notice if there are specific individuals or situations that consistently leave you feeling disempowered. Awareness is the first step to change.

2. Establish and Maintain Boundaries

- **Clear Boundaries:** Clearly define your emotional and physical boundaries. Know what is acceptable to you and what is not in terms of how others treat you and affect your energy.

- **Communicate Boundaries:** Assertively communicate your boundaries to others. Be direct yet respectful in letting people know how you expect to be treated.

3. Protect Your Energy

- **Visualization Techniques:** Use visualization techniques to create a protective shield around you. Imagine a bubble or cloak of light that keeps negative energies out while allowing positive energies to flow freely.

- **Grounding Practices:** Engage in grounding practices that connect you with the earth and your own center. Techniques such as walking barefoot on grass, meditation, and deep breathing can help stabilize your energy.

4. Cultivate Positive Energy

- Surround Yourself with Positivity: **Spend time with people who uplift you and engage in activities that nourish your soul. Positive environments and relationships can bolster your energy and resilience.**
- Practice Gratitude: **Cultivate a habit of gratitude. Focusing on what you are thankful for can shift your energy from being reactive to others' negativity to proactively creating your own positivity.**

5. Strengthen Personal Empowerment

- Self-Care: **Prioritize self-care. Engaging in activities that promote your well-being strengthens your energy field and your ability to stand firm in your power.**
- Develop Personal Strengths: **Work on developing your personal strengths and capabilities. Knowing your worth and believing in your abilities makes you less susceptible to being overpowered by others.**

6. Seek Support

- Professional Guidance: If you find it challenging to manage the impact of others' energies on your own, consider seeking support from a counselor, therapist, or energy healing practitioner.
- Community: Connect with supportive communities, whether online or in-person, where you can share experiences and learn from others who have faced similar challenges.

7. Regular Energy Cleansing

- Energy Cleansing Practices: Regularly cleanse your energy field using practices such as sage smudging, salt baths, or energy healing techniques like Reiki. These practices can help clear any negative energies you may have absorbed.

Countering the effects of others' energy control or overpowerment is an ongoing process of self-care, boundary maintenance, and personal growth. By becoming more attuned to your own energy and taking proactive steps to protect and empower yourself, you can navigate your interactions with others more effectively, maintaining your equilibrium and autonomy in the face of external influences.

Identifying Techniques

- Reflection and Journaling: Regular reflection and journaling can help bring to light hidden beliefs, fears, and traumas that serve as blockages. Writing down thoughts, feelings, and experiences provides clarity and insight into patterns that may not be immediately apparent.

- Mindfulness and Meditation: Practices that cultivate mindfulness and meditation can quiet the mind and heighten awareness, allowing for a clearer perception of internal blockages. They can also facilitate a deeper connection with one's intuition, which can guide the identification of these hindrances.

- Body Awareness: Often, our bodies hold onto emotional and energetic blockages in the form of tension or discomfort. Practices like yoga, Tai Chi, or even simple body scanning techniques can help identify areas where blockages might be stored physically.

- Seeking Feedback: Sometimes, it can be beneficial to seek feedback from trusted friends, family, or professionals who might offer insights into blockages that one may not be able to see.
- Energy Work: Engaging in energy work with a skilled practitioner, such as Reiki, acupuncture, or chakra balancing, can help identify and clear energetic blockages, facilitating a smoother manifestation process.

Identifying blockages is a profound and sometimes challenging journey into the self. It requires honesty, vulnerability, and a willingness to confront and heal aspects of oneself that may be uncomfortable. However, this process is integral to personal growth and the manifestation of one's true desires. By acknowledging and addressing these blockages, you open the door to a more aligned, abundant, and fulfilled existence.

Navigating Through Disappointment

Navigating Through Disappointment delves into the inevitable moments of setback and disillusionment that can accompany the journey of manifestation. Despite our best efforts, intentions, and practices, there will be times when outcomes don't align with our desires, leading to feelings of disappointment. This phase of the manifestation process is crucial for the growth, learning, and recalibration of our goals and strategies. Understanding how to move through disappointment constructively can transform these experiences into valuable lessons and stepping stones toward future success.

Acknowledging and Embracing Disappointment

- Allow Yourself to Feel: The first step in navigating through disappointment is to acknowledge and allow yourself to feel the emotions that come with it. Suppressing or denying these feelings can lead to further emotional blockages. Instead, give yourself permission to experience disappointment, understanding it as a natural response to unmet expectations.

- Self-Compassion: Practicing self-compassion is crucial during times of disappointment. Be kind to yourself, recognizing that setbacks are a part of the human experience and do not define your worth or capabilities.

Gaining Perspective

- Reframe the Experience: Instead of viewing disappointment as a failure, try to reframe it as an opportunity for growth and learning. Ask yourself what can be learned from the situation and how it can inform your future actions and decisions.
- Seek the Silver Lining: Often, within disappointment, there are hidden blessings or lessons that can lead to new paths or solutions we hadn't considered. Look for the silver lining, focusing on any positive aspects or insights gained from the experience.

Understanding Your Trauma

Understanding your trauma is a critical step in the manifestation journey. Trauma, whether stemming from a single event or a series of ongoing situations, can deeply impact one's emotional, psychological, and even physical well-being. It often creates blockages that can prevent individuals from fully engaging with their desires and harnessing the power of manifestation.

The Nature of Trauma

Trauma can vary widely from person to person; what deeply affects one individual may not impact another in the same way. It's not just the event itself but the individual's emotional and psychological response to it. Trauma can result from experiences such as abuse, loss, accidents, natural disasters, and other distressing events. It can lead to feelings of fear, helplessness, or horror, challenging one's sense of safety and stability.

The Impact of Trauma on Manifestation

- Limiting Beliefs: **Trauma often instills deep-seated limiting beliefs about oneself, others, and the world— such as feelings of unworthiness, fear of rejection, or a deep-seated belief that one doesn't deserve happiness or success.**

- Emotional Blockages: **Unprocessed emotions related to trauma can create blockages. These emotional barriers can hinder one's ability to visualize and manifest their desires as they keep the individual stuck in past pain.**

- Energetic Imbalances: **Trauma can lead to imbalances in one's energetic body, affecting one's vibration and ability to align with positive experiences and outcomes.**

Addressing and Healing Trauma

- Awareness and Acknowledgment: **The first step in healing is acknowledging the trauma and its impact on your life. This involves facing the painful emotions and memories you may have been avoiding.**

- Seeking Professional Support: Therapy or counseling can be incredibly beneficial in processing trauma. Professionals can offer guidance, support, and strategies for healing.

- Body-Centered Practices: Activities like yoga, meditation, and breathing exercises can help release trauma stored in the body and promote emotional balance.

- Self-Compassion and Forgiveness: Practicing self-compassion and working toward forgiveness (of oneself and others) can be powerful tools in the healing process. They help release bitterness and open up new possibilities.

- Building a Supportive Community: Connecting with supportive individuals who understand and empathize with your journey can provide comfort and encouragement.

Integrating

Integrating the concept of major life stages with the impact of trauma provides a nuanced understanding of how pivotal moments in our development can be significantly influenced by traumatic experiences. Trauma, whether it's a singular event or a series of events, can deeply affect an individual's psychosocial development, influencing their decisions, behaviors, and overall life trajectory. Here's a closer look at how trauma can intersect with Erik Erikson's psychosocial stages of development, potentially affecting the natural progression and resolution of key conflicts at various life stages:

1. Adolescence (around 12-18 years)

- Trauma Impact: **Traumatic experiences during adolescence, such as bullying, abuse, or the loss of a loved one, can profoundly affect identity formation. This may lead to confusion, withdrawal, or risky behaviors as teenagers struggle to find their place in the world. The quest for identity could be overshadowed by efforts to cope with trauma, potentially leading to delayed or distorted development of a coherent sense of self.**

2. Young Adulthood (around 19-40 years)

- Trauma Impact: **Trauma in young adulthood can disrupt the formation of intimate relationships and lead to isolation. Early adulthood traumas, such as relationship violence, trauma in combat, or significant life failures, can hinder the ability to form close, trusting relationships with others. This might manifest in avoidance of intimacy, difficulty in maintaining relationships, or the repetition of traumatic relationship patterns.**

3. Midlife (around 40-65 years)

- Trauma Impact: **Trauma experienced directly or indirectly during midlife can precipitate a crisis that intensifies the reflective nature of this stage. Individuals may struggle with unresolved trauma from earlier stages, leading to significant life reassessments and sometimes drastic changes in relationships, careers, and personal goals. For some, this period may involve confronting and healing from past traumas to move forward.**

4. Retirement Age (65 years and older)

- Trauma Impact: **The transition into retirement can reopen past traumas or introduce new ones, such as the loss of peers, facing one's mortality, or feeling a lack of purpose. For some, retirement may offer the time and space to address past traumas through reflection or therapy, while for others, it may bring about feelings of regret or unresolved trauma, impacting their sense of fulfillment and purpose.**

Navigating Trauma Across Life Stages

Understanding the intersection between life stages and trauma emphasizes the need for sensitive approaches to trauma at every stage of development. It highlights the importance of:

- Trauma-Informed Care: **Implementing approaches that recognize the widespread impact of trauma and paths for recovery throughout the lifespan.**

- Resilience Building: **Encouraging the development of resilience and coping mechanisms to navigate life transitions and traumas more effectively.**
- Continuous Support: **Offering ongoing emotional and psychological support to address trauma's effects, acknowledging that healing is a continuous process that may require attention at various life stages.**

Recognizing the pivotal periods in life stages alongside the potential impact of trauma can help individuals and professionals develop more tailored strategies for intervention, support, and healing. It underscores the importance of addressing trauma to ensure that each individual has the opportunity to navigate life's transitions smoothly, making informed decisions that align with their evolving goals and values despite past adversities.

Emotions

Trauma exerts a profound influence on our emotions, behaviors, and ultimately our ability to manifest our desires and ambitions. At its core, trauma disrupts our emotional equilibrium, shaping our perceptions of the world, ourselves, and our potential futures. This disruption can significantly impact the manifestation process, which relies heavily on emotional alignment, clear intentions, and positive action toward desired outcomes. Understanding the dynamics of trauma's influence on our emotions and manifestation capabilities provides insight into navigating these challenges more effectively.

Emotional Dysregulation and Its Impact

- Hyperarousal and Hypervigilance: **Trauma can lead to a** state of constant alertness to threats, real or imagined. This hyperarousal and hypervigilance consume considerable emotional and physical energy, leaving less capacity for positive focus and manifestation efforts.

- Anxiety and Fear: **Trauma often breeds anxiety and** fear, emotions that can cloud judgment and hinder the ability to envision a positive future. The presence of these emotions can attract more of the same, according to the law of attraction, complicating efforts to manifest positive experiences.

- Depression and Hopelessness: The weight of traumatic experiences can lead to feelings of depression and a pervasive sense of hopelessness. These feelings directly counteract the optimism and belief in possibility that are central to the manifestation process.

Impact on Manifestation

- Distorted Beliefs and Expectations: Trauma can distort one's beliefs about what is possible, deserving, or achievable, leading to lowered expectations and diminished desires. This can severely limit what one feels capable of manifesting.
- Focus on Negative Outcomes: Trauma survivors may find themselves focusing more on avoiding further pain or reliving past traumas rather than pursuing positive goals or outcomes. This focus on negative potentialities can inadvertently attract more negative experiences.

- Challenges in Emotional Alignment: **Manifestation requires aligning one's emotional state with one's desires. Trauma can make it difficult to maintain the positive emotional states necessary for effective manifestation, as past pain might overshadow present positivity.**

Navigating Trauma for Effective Manifestation

- Healing and Processing Trauma: **Engaging in trauma-informed therapy, mindfulness practices, and emotional healing techniques can help address the root causes of emotional dysregulation. Healing from trauma creates space for more positive emotions and beliefs to emerge.**
- Rebuilding Trust and Safety: **Establishing a sense of safety within oneself is crucial. Practices that foster self-compassion, self-trust, and a sense of internal safety can gradually replace fear and anxiety with confidence and peace.**
- Refocusing on Desires: **As emotional regulation improves, it becomes easier to refocus on one's desires and aspirations. Setting small, achievable goals can**

help rebuild the belief in one's ability to manifest and achieve positive outcomes.

- Visualization and Affirmation: Using visualization techniques to imagine a future free from the constraints of past trauma, combined with affirmations that reinforce one's worthiness and capability, can realign emotional and energetic states toward manifestation.

The impact of trauma on our emotions represents a significant challenge to our ability to manifest our desires. However, by acknowledging and addressing the influence of trauma, individuals can embark on a healing journey that not only mitigates these impacts but also empowers them to reclaim their ability to manifest a fulfilling and abundant life. Understanding the interplay between trauma, emotions, and manifestation is a crucial step in this transformative process, offering a pathway through which individuals can navigate from the shadows of their past traumas into the light of their desired futures.

Healing from trauma is not merely a pathway to recovery; it's a vital step toward unlocking the full potential of manifestation. The journey is deeply personal, often challenging, yet undeniably essential for removing the emotional and energetic blockages that trauma imposes on us. By addressing and healing these wounds, we align our energy more closely with our desires, setting the stage for a life of abundance that is not just a possibility but a reality within our grasp.

The profound impact of trauma on our emotions—on how we perceive ourselves, our world, and our potential—can significantly deter our manifestation capabilities. It can lead us to focus more on avoiding further pain than on pursuing our true desires. This state of being can inadvertently attract more of the negative experiences we wish to avoid. However, by confronting and processing our trauma, we begin to dismantle these barriers, gradually shifting our focus from past pain to future aspirations.

Empowering Transformation Through Healing

Understanding and healing your trauma does more than liberate you from the chains of past pain; it opens doors to a future ripe with opportunities, abundance, and joy. This healing journey is the cornerstone of genuine manifestation. It empowers you to co-create with the universe from a place of strength, clarity, and emotional alignment.

Healing encourages a reevaluation of your beliefs about what you deserve and what you can achieve, allowing you to dream bigger and aim higher. It involves rebuilding trust and safety within yourself and fostering an environment where positive emotions can flourish. These shifts are critical for aligning your vibrational energy with your desires, facilitating a manifestation process that is not hindered by the weight of unprocessed trauma.

A Call to Action for Co-Creation

As you heal, you'll find that manifesting your desires becomes less about overcoming barriers and more about effortless co-creation with the universe. This doesn't mean the journey will be free from challenges, but rather that you'll be equipped with the resilience, understanding, and emotional freedom to navigate these challenges effectively.

Integrating healing into your manifestation practice sets the stage for a life that mirrors your truest desires and potential and contributes to a cycle of continuous growth, empowerment, and fulfillment. Therefore, the journey of healing from trauma is not just a prerequisite for practical manifestation but a transformative process that enriches your entire being, enabling you to co-create a life that is not only desired but deeply deserved.

Transforming Blockages into Stepping Stones

Transforming Blockages into Stepping Stones reframes the challenges and obstacles encountered on the manifestation journey as opportunities for growth, learning, and deeper self-awareness. Rather than perceiving blockages as insurmountable barriers, this perspective encourages viewing them as integral parts of the journey, each with valuable lessons that pave the way for future success and enlightenment. This transformative approach facilitates the manifestation process and enriches personal development.

Recognizing the Value in Blockages

- **Lessons in Disguise:** Every blockage, no matter how daunting, carries a lesson or insight. Identifying and understanding these lessons can illuminate aspects of ourselves or our approach that need adjustment or healing.

- **Signals for Reevaluation:** Blockages often signal that something within our approach, mindset, or intention may be misaligned with our highest good. They prompt us to pause, reflect, and reassess our path, ensuring that our desires are truly in harmony with our soul's purpose.

Strategies for Transformation

- **Mindful Reflection:** Engage in practices like meditation, journaling, or quiet contemplation to explore the root causes of blockages. This introspection can reveal underlying beliefs, fears, or patterns that need addressing.

- **Embrace Adaptability:** Cultivate a mindset of flexibility and openness to change. Sometimes, the way forward involves adapting our goals, exploring new strategies, or even pivoting in a completely different direction.

- Seek Support and Guidance: Don't hesitate to seek support from mentors, counselors, or spiritual guides. External perspectives can offer invaluable insights and tools for overcoming blockages.

- Practice Forgiveness: Forgiveness, both of self and others, can release the emotional weight of past experiences or perceived failures. This release is crucial for moving past blockages and opening up to new possibilities.

Applying the Lessons Learned

- Incorporate New Insights: Use the insights gained from overcoming blockages to refine your manifestation practices. This may involve setting clearer intentions, adopting new visualization techniques, or strengthening your emotional and energetic alignment.

- Celebrate Progress: Recognize and celebrate each step forward, no matter how small. Acknowledging progress reinforces your ability to overcome obstacles and build momentum.

- Build Resilience: Each blockage transformed into a stepping stone strengthens resilience, deepening your trust in yourself and the manifestation process. This resilience becomes a powerful asset for navigating future challenges.

Transforming blockages into stepping stones is a dynamic process that underscores the manifestation journey's inherently evolutionary nature. It shifts the narrative from one of struggle against obstacles to one of engagement with opportunities for growth and self-discovery. By embracing and learning from blockages, we not only facilitate the manifestation of our desires but also embark on a profound journey of personal transformation. This journey enhances our capacity for co-creation, aligns us more closely with our highest aspirations, and ultimately leads to a richer, more fulfilling life experience.

"Illuminating and Overcoming Your Shadows"
Reflect on a time when you felt blocked in your manifestation efforts. What was the blockage, and how did you address it?

Strengthening Your Faith and Trust

Strengthening Your Faith and Trust delves into the essential elements of belief and confidence, not just in the universe or a higher power but in oneself and the journey of manifestation. Faith and trust are the bedrock upon which successful manifestation is built, acting as the fuel that propels desires from the realm of thought into reality. Cultivating a deep, unwavering sense of faith and trust can significantly enhance the manifestation process, providing the resilience and optimism needed to navigate the ups and downs of bringing one's dreams to fruition.

Understanding the Role of Faith and Trust

- **Faith in the Process:** Believing in the manifestation process itself is crucial. This means trusting that the universe (or however one conceptualizes the greater force) is always working in your favor, even when immediate circumstances seem contrary.
- **Trust in Timing:** An integral part of faith is trust in divine timing. Understanding that manifestations may not unfold according to your timeline but rather in

alignment with a pearl of greater wisdom can ease anxiety and impatience.

- Self-Belief: Equally important is faith in oneself. This encompasses confidence in one's abilities, worthiness of desires, and the right to manifest one's aspirations.

Strategies for Strengthening Faith and Trust

- Mindfulness and Meditation: Regular meditation can quiet the mind, allowing for a clearer connection with the universe and oneself. Mindfulness practices can help maintain a state of openness and receptivity, fostering trust in the journey.
- Affirmations and Visualization: Positive affirmations can reinforce trust and faith, especially when focused on the certainty of outcomes and one's ability to co-create with the universe. Visualization techniques, where one imagines the successful realization of desires, can also bolster belief in the manifestation process.
- Journaling and Reflective Practices: Keeping a journal of one's thoughts, feelings, and the synchronicities or signs that appear along the way can provide tangible

evidence of the universe's responsiveness, reinforcing faith and trust.

- Gratitude: Practicing gratitude daily for both the seen and unseen support received can amplify faith in the benevolence of the universe and the efficacy of one's manifestation efforts.

- Community and Shared Experiences: Engaging with a community of like-minded individuals can offer support, share experiences of faith and trust, and celebrate the manifestation journeys of its members, thereby strengthening individual and collective belief.

Nurturing Faith and Trust During Challenges

- Revisiting Successes: Remind yourself of past successes and how faith and trust played a role in those achievements. This can serve as a reminder that challenges are temporary and that you have the strength to overcome them.

- Seek Inspiration: Reading or listening to stories of successful manifestations can inspire and reinforce faith and trust during times of doubt.

- **Surrender and Release Control:** Learning to surrender and release the need for control can alleviate the pressure of manifestation, allowing space for the universe to work in mysterious and often unexpected ways.

Strengthening your faith and trust is an ongoing practice that enhances not only your ability to manifest but also your overall spiritual well-being. By cultivating a deep sense of belief in the universe, trust in the timing of your life, and confidence in your capabilities, you create a solid foundation for your desires to materialize. Faith and trust transform the journey of manifestation into a more joyous and fulfilling experience, reminding us that we are never alone in our endeavors and that the universe conspires in our favor.

Moving Forward

- **Adjust and Realign:** Based on the insights gained from your disappointment, consider adjusting your goals, methods, or mindset. This may involve setting new intentions, adopting different strategies, or shifting your perspective on what success looks like.

- Recommit to Your Journey: Disappointment can sometimes lead to a loss of motivation or faith in the manifestation process. Once you've processed your emotions and gained perspective, recommit to your journey with a renewed sense of purpose and clarity. Remember, every step, even backward ones, is a part of your path to growth.

- Maintain a Gratitude Practice: Cultivating gratitude, even in the face of disappointment, can shift your focus from what's lacking to what's abundant in your life. This shift in perspective can lighten the weight of disappointment and open your heart to future possibilities.

Navigating through disappointment is an integral aspect of the manifestation journey. It tests our resilience, teaches us valuable lessons, and, most importantly, offers us the chance to deepen our understanding of ourselves and our desires. By approaching disappointment with grace, patience, and a willingness to learn, we transform these experiences into catalysts for personal growth and manifestation mastery. Remember, each disappointment is not an end but a bend in the road, guiding us toward our true paths and the fulfillment of our deepest aspirations.

"Learning from Life's Hurdles"

Identify a major obstacle you've encountered on your manifestation journey. How did you overcome it, and what did you learn from the experience?

Part VIII: Clarity and Intention: Communicating with the Universe

The Language of the Universe

Clarity and Intention: Communicating with the Universe delves into the nuanced art of engaging with the universe in a manner that aligns with one's deepest desires and aspirations. It emphasizes the importance of clarity and intention in the manifestation process, exploring how these elements serve as the primary language through which we communicate our wishes to the universe. This section sheds light on the subtle yet profound ways in which the universe receives and responds to our signals, guiding us toward a deeper understanding of co-creation and the power of our thoughts and intentions.

The Essence of Clarity

- Defining Desires Precisely: Clarity involves being explicit about what you want to manifest. Vague desires can lead to mixed signals, making it challenging for the universe to deliver what you truly seek. Detailed visualization and specific goal-setting are tools that help crystallize your desires, enhancing the universe's ability to comprehend and fulfill them.

- The Power of Words: Words carry energy and intention. Using affirmative language that embodies certainty and positivity when articulating your desires amplifies the clarity of your message to the universe.

The Role of Intention

- Setting Purposeful Intentions: Intention is the soul behind the desire, the why that drives what you wish to manifest. It imbues your goals with depth and purpose, ensuring your desires align with your highest good and the greater good.

- Consistency and Continuity: Holding a steady intention, even in the face of obstacles, signals to the universe your commitment and sincerity, acting as a beacon that guides the manifestation process.

Communicating with the Universe

- Synchronicities as Responses: The universe often communicates back through synchronicities— meaningful coincidences that appear in our lives as signs, guidance, or affirmation of our path. Recognizing and interpreting these synchronicities requires an open heart and an attentive mind.
- Emotional Resonance: Emotions are a potent form of communication with the universe. Joy, passion, and gratitude are frequencies that resonate deeply with the fabric of the universe, attracting similar energies and experiences.

Enhancing the Dialogue

- Meditation and Silence: In the silence of meditation, the chatter of the mind subsides, allowing for a clearer channel of communication between you and the universe. This quietude is fertile ground for receiving insights, inspiration, and guidance.
- Rituals and Symbolism: Creating personal rituals or using symbols that hold special meaning can enhance your connection to the universe, making the act of communication more profound and personalized.
- Journaling as Reflection: Writing down your thoughts, intentions, and experiences with manifestation creates a reflective space to explore your relationship with the universe, offering insights into the effectiveness of your communication.

Clarity and intention are the keystones of communicating with the universe, the language through which we express our desires and open ourselves to receiving guidance and blessings. By articulating our desires with precision and purpose, we invite the universe to respond, co-creating our reality in harmony with a deeper cosmic order. This part of the journey underscores the importance of being deliberate and mindful in our interactions with the universe, fostering a dialogue that is enriched with clarity, intention, and mutual understanding.

"Sustaining Your Co-Created Success"

Consider a manifestation that has had a long-lasting impact on your life. How do you continue to nurture and maintain this abundance?

The Chaos of Unclear Thoughts

The Chaos of Unclear Thoughts delves into the turbulence and confusion that can arise when our internal dialogue lacks clarity and direction. In the context of manifestation and our interaction with the universe, unclear thoughts create a foggy landscape, hindering our ability to co-create effectively and leading to outcomes that may not align with our deepest desires. This section explores the implications of such mental chaos and offers insights into navigating back to a state of clarity and purpose.

The Impact of Unclear Thoughts

- Muddled Manifestations: When our thoughts are unclear, the signals we send to the universe are equally ambiguous. This can result in manifestations that are misaligned with our true intentions or desires, reflecting the disorder rather than the clear outcomes we hope for.
- Emotional Dissonance: The chaos of unclear thoughts often breeds emotional turmoil. Feelings of frustration, anxiety, and disconnection can surface, further

clouding our mental landscape and complicating our emotional and energetic alignment with the universe.

- Stagnation and Confusion: Without clear thoughts and intentions, it can be challenging to take decisive action toward our goals. This can lead to a sense of stagnation, where progress feels halted, and the path forward appears obscured.

Navigating Through Mental Chaos

- Seeking Stillness: Creating moments of stillness through meditation, mindfulness, or simply being in nature can help quiet the mind. In the silence, the dust of confusion can settle, allowing for clearer thoughts to emerge.
- Clarification Practices: Engaging in practices aimed at clarifying thoughts can be immensely beneficial. This could include journaling, speaking with a trusted advisor or therapist, or using visualization techniques to hone in on what you truly desire.
- Embracing Simplicity: Sometimes, the key to overcoming the chaos of unclear thoughts is to simplify. Focusing on one thought, intention, or goal at

a time can prevent the overwhelm that contributes to mental chaos.

The Power of Directed Thought

- Intention Setting: Clear, directed thought begins with setting precise, well-defined intentions. Identifying what you truly want—not just on a superficial level but at the core of your being—can illuminate your path and focus your mental energy.
- Affirmations: Regularly affirming your intentions and desires with positive, decisive language reinforces clarity. Affirmations act as mental signposts, keeping you aligned with your goals amidst the noise of competing thoughts.
- Feedback Loops: Pay attention to the feedback you receive from the universe in the form of synchronicities, feelings, and manifestations. This feedback can guide you in refining your thoughts and intentions, steering you away from chaos toward coherence.

The chaos of unclear thoughts presents a significant challenge on the journey of manifestation, but it also offers an opportunity for growth and self-discovery. By recognizing the impact of mental clarity on our ability to manifest, we can take deliberate steps to cultivate a clear, focused mind. In doing so, we enhance our co-creative partnership with the universe and move closer to realizing our true potential and bringing our deepest desires into reality. Overcoming the chaos and finding clarity is a transformative process that aligns us more closely with our authentic selves and the universal flow.

Crafting Your Desires

Crafting Your Desires focuses on the deliberate and intentional process of defining and shaping what you truly want to bring into your life. It's a creative and reflective practice that goes beyond surface-level wants, digging deep into your core values, aspirations, and the essence of what brings you fulfillment and joy. This careful articulation of desires is crucial for effective manifestation, as it ensures that what you seek to attract aligns with your highest self and contributes positively to your journey of growth and happiness.

Understanding the Depth of Desire

- Self-Exploration: **Begin with introspection. Ask yourself what you truly desire and why. This exploration should delve into how these desires resonate with your core values and how they contribute to your sense of purpose and fulfillment.**
- Differentiating Needs from Wants: **Distinguish between fleeting wants and deeper needs. True desires often fulfill an inner need for growth, expression, connection, or fulfillment, whereas wants may be more superficial or externally influenced.**

The Process of Crafting

- Visualization: **Engage in visualization exercises where you vividly imagine your life with your desires manifested. Consider how they impact your daily living, relationships, personal growth, and overall happiness.**
- Specificity and Detail: **Be as specific and detailed as possible when defining your desires. The universe responds to clarity. Detailed descriptions of what you**

wish to manifest allow for a more focused and directed energy in the manifestation process.

- Alignment Check: Ensure that each desire is in alignment with your higher self and not just a response to societal expectations or external pressures. Desires that truly resonate with your authentic self are more powerful and fulfilling.

Tools and Techniques

- Journaling: Writing down your desires can help clarify and solidify them in your mind and heart. It also serves as a tangible record to revisit and refine over time.
- Affirmations: Create positive affirmations that encapsulate your desires. Repeating these affirmations can help embed them in your subconscious, reinforcing your intention and belief in their manifestation.
- Mood Boards: Visual representations of your desires, such as mood boards or vision boards, can be powerful tools for keeping your intentions clear and front of mind. They serve as daily visual reminders of what you're working toward.

Maintaining Flexibility

- Openness to Evolution: **Recognize that as you grow and change, your desires may also evolve. Stay open to this evolution, and be willing to adjust your aspirations as you gain new insights and experiences.**

- Detachment from Specific Outcomes: **While it's important to be clear about what you want, it's equally crucial to detach from rigid expectations about how and when these desires will manifest. Trust the process and remain open to the universe's timing and wisdom.**

Crafting Your Desires is a foundational step in the manifestation journey, requiring deep self-reflection, clarity, and intention. By understanding the true nature of your desires, specifying them in detail, and ensuring they align with your authentic self, you create a powerful blueprint for manifestation. This intentional approach enhances your co-creative abilities and ensures that the manifestations you attract are in harmony with your highest good, enriching your life with genuine fulfillment and joy.

Sending Clear Signals

Sending Clear Signals to the universe is a pivotal aspect of the manifestation process. It involves articulating your desires in a way that is unambiguous and aligned, ensuring that the intentions you set forth are received without distortion. This clarity acts like a beacon, cutting through the noise of everyday life and aligning your energy with the frequencies of your desires. Achieving this level of clarity and coherence in your communication with the universe amplifies your ability to co-create your reality.

The Importance of Clarity

- Reduces Misinterpretation: Clear signals minimize the chances of misinterpretation by the universe. Just as in human communication, clarity in your intentions prevents misunderstandings, focusing your manifestational energy like a laser beam.
- Enhances Vibrational Alignment: The clearer your signal, the more precisely your energy aligns with that of your desire. This alignment is crucial for attracting what you truly want into your life.

Techniques for Sending Clear Signals

- Detailed Visualization: Engage in detailed visualization exercises where you not only see the outcome but also involve all your senses. Imagine touching, hearing, smelling, and even tasting the success of your desire. The more detailed your visualization, the clearer the signal.
- Affirmative Language: Use affirmative language that is present-tense and positive. Instead of focusing on what you don't want, articulate what you do want. Phrases like "I am" or "I have" send strong signals of already being in possession of or embodying your desires.
- Emotional Charging: Emotions are powerful signal boosters. When setting intentions or visualizing, infuse your thoughts with strong, positive emotions. The emotional charge behind your desires sends a clear and potent signal to the universe.
- Consistency and Repetition: Consistently sending your intentions through regular practice (such as daily affirmations, visualization sessions, or manifestation

rituals) reinforces the clarity of your signal. Repetition is key to maintaining a clear and ongoing communication channel with the universe.

Avoiding Mixed Signals

- Identify and Release Contradictory Beliefs: Contradictory beliefs or fears can muddle your signal. Identify any beliefs that counter your desires and work on releasing them. Techniques like journaling, meditation, or even professional therapy can aid in this process.

- Focus on One Clear Outcome at a Time: While you may have multiple desires, focusing on one clear outcome at a time can help prevent mixed signals. Once you feel aligned and clear about one desire, you can then shift your focus to another.

- Mindful of Your Environment: Your environment and the people you interact with can influence the clarity of your signals. Surround yourself with positivity and support to reinforce the clarity and strength of your intentions.

Sending Clear Signals is an art and a discipline that enhances your manifestational abilities. It requires mindfulness, precision, and emotional investment. Ensuring that your desires are communicated to the universe with utmost clarity and vibrational alignment will pave the way for a more effective and fulfilling co-creative process. Remember, the universe is always listening, ready to respond to your clear, focused, and heartfelt calls.

Command and Demand

The concept of "command and demand" in the context of spiritual manifestation reflects a potent, unwavering form of expression rooted in absolute faith and authority. This approach is reminiscent of the way Jesus is depicted in various religious texts, where his words and actions carry the power of unequivocal belief and the certainty of immediate manifestation. He spoke and acted with a deep-seated knowledge that what he commanded would come to pass without hesitation or doubt. This principle can be applied to the manifestation process, emphasizing the importance of clarity, intention, and the strength of one's conviction.

The Power of Command

- Authority Over Doubt: Commanding rather than simply asking or hoping is a practice of asserting authority over one's circumstances, doubts, and the external environment. It signifies a profound level of self-belief and understanding of one's co-creative power with the universe.

- Immediate Action: Command in this context also implies an expectation of immediate action or change. It's the belief in the now, not in a distant, uncertain future. This immediacy underscores the practitioner's confidence in their manifestation power.

The Role of Demand

- Clarity and Precision: Demanding is about being precise and clear about what is wanted, leaving no room for ambiguity. It is a declaration of one's desires with the expectation that they will be fulfilled.

- Unwavering Faith: The act of demanding spiritual manifestation is backed by unwavering faith. It's a testament to the individual's unshakable trust in the universe or higher power to deliver what is being asked for, rooted in a deep understanding of one's deservingness and alignment with one's desires.

Incorporating Command and Demand in Manifestation

- Affirmative Language: Use language that is definitive and affirmative. Speak as though what you are manifesting is already yours, affirming your desires with certainty and conviction.
- Visualize with Authority: When visualizing, do so with the authority of knowing that what you seek is already on its way to you. Imagine your desires manifesting in the present, feeling the emotions and sensations as if they are already part of your reality.
- Act As If: Live your life as if what you are commanding and demanding has already manifested. This doesn't mean living beyond your means but adopting the mindset, behaviors, and emotional state congruent with your desires being fulfilled.

Balancing Command with Surrender

While the approach of command and demand is powerful, it is also essential to balance it with the art of surrender. Surrendering isn't about giving up on your desires but acknowledging that the universe might have a broader perspective. It's about trusting that, while you command and demand with authority, the universe will deliver in the way that's most aligned with your highest good, even if it doesn't match your expectations to the letter.

Commanding and demanding in the context of manifestation is an expression of profound faith, certainty, and the active exertion of one's will in co-creation with the universe. It requires a balance of assertiveness, clarity, and surrender— holding strong to your desires while remaining open to the universe's wisdom in fulfilling them. This approach, inspired by figures like Jesus, highlights the power of spoken words and the importance of embodying the certainty and immediacy of manifestation in one's attitude and actions.

Staying In Your Power

Staying in your power, especially in the face of others who may attempt to control or diminish your energy, is vital to maintaining your integrity, boundaries, and sense of self. It involves recognizing your strength and value, regardless of external pressures or attempts to sway your direction, emotions, or choices. This resilience is crucial not only for personal well-being but also for manifesting your true desires without interference. Here's how to stay in your power amidst external attempts at control.

Recognizing External Energy Control

- Identify Attempts at Control: Be aware of the various forms in which attempts to control or influence your energy can manifest. This could be through manipulation, coercion, excessive criticism, or even unsolicited advice that doesn't align with your inner truth.
- Understand Your Triggers: Knowing what triggers you to feel disempowered or vulnerable can help you prepare and protect your energy. Awareness allows

you to approach such situations with a strategy rather than being caught off guard.

Strategies for Staying in Your Power

- Firm Boundaries: Establish and communicate clear boundaries with others. Boundaries inform others of what is acceptable to you, safeguarding your energy from being manipulated or drained.
- Self-Awareness and Reflection: Cultivate a deep understanding of your values, goals, and what truly matters to you. This self-awareness acts as an anchor, keeping you rooted in your power even when external forces attempt to sway you.
- Assertive Communication: Practice expressing your needs, thoughts, and feelings confidently and clearly. Assertive communication respects both your own boundaries and those of others, ensuring that your energy is not overrun by someone else's agenda.
- Emotional Regulation: Learn techniques to manage your emotional responses. Meditation, breathing exercises, and mindfulness can help you maintain calm

and centeredness, preventing others from easily disrupting your emotional state.

Empowering Practices

- Energy Cleansing: **Regularly engage in practices that cleanse your energy field, such as meditating, spending time in nature, or using sage or crystals. These practices can help remove any negativity or external influences that have attached to you.**
- Seek Supportive Communities: **Surround yourself with people who uplift and support you. A community that recognizes and honors your power can reinforce your ability to stand strong in your energy.**
- Self-Care and Nourishment: **Prioritize self-care to reinforce your energy and resilience. You're better equipped to maintain your power when you're well-rested, nourished, and fulfilled.**

Reclaiming Your Power

- Visualization: Use visualization techniques to imagine a shield of protective energy around you, repelling any attempts to control or diminish your power.
- Affirmations: Regularly affirm your strength, worth, and the right to own your space. Positive affirmations can fortify your internal power, making it harder for external energies to impact you.
- Learning from Interactions: Reflect on interactions that challenge your power, seeking lessons and strengths you can draw from them. Each challenge is an opportunity for growth and reaffirmation of your resilience.

Staying in your power when others try to control your energy is a testament to your strength, self-awareness, and commitment to your path. By recognizing external attempts at control, reinforcing your boundaries, and engaging in practices that nourish and protect your energy, you ensure that you remain the master of your journey. This steadfastness guards your well-being and empowers you to manifest your true desires free from undue influence.

"Clarifying Your Dialogue with the Universe"

How clear are your current intentions with the universe, and what steps can you take to refine and clarify them further?

Rediscovering The Path to Abundance

Rediscovering the Path to Abundance involves a journey of reflection, realignment, and recommitment to the principles and practices that guide us toward manifesting our desires. It's not uncommon for individuals to stray from their path, losing sight of their goals and the conversations with the universe that once guided them. This deviation can result from various factors—life's unpredictability, changing circumstances, or simply the human tendency to drift from our disciplined practices over time. The key to finding your way back lies in identifying where the disconnect occurred, particularly in the context of the 5-step manifestation process: Unconscious Thought, Conscious Thought, Action, Manifestation, and Emotional Response.

Pinpointing the Disconnect

Many find that their divergence from the path to abundance relates directly to their goals and their communication with the universe. This might manifest as inconsistency in expressing desires—what is sought from the universe one week might shift dramatically by the next week, month, or year, creating a cacophony of mixed signals that muddies the waters of manifestation. This inconsistency can cloud your trajectory toward abundance, leaving your original plans adrift.

The Importance of Clarity and Consistency

Regaining clarity and consistency in your intentions is paramount. Reflect on each of the five steps to see where the misalignment occurred. Ask yourself:

- Unconscious Thought: **Have fleeting desires been mistaken for true goals?**
- Conscious Thought: **Have your consistent, focused thoughts on your desires wavered?**
- Action: **Have you faltered in taking deliberate steps toward your goals?**
- Manifestation: **Have you observed manifestations but failed to recognize or acknowledge them, perhaps due to their subtlety or unexpected form?**

- Emotional Response: How have your emotional reactions to achieved or unachieved goals influenced your journey?

Realigning with Your Path

Once you've identified where the misstep occurred, the next step is realigning with your path. This realignment involves:

- Revisiting Your Goals: Take time to reassess and clarify your goals. Ensure they are still aligned with your true desires and the life you want to lead.
- Clear Communication with the Universe: Refine how you communicate your goals to the universe. Establish a consistent practice of expressing your desires clearly and regularly, whether through visualization, affirmation, or written intention.
- Setting Time-Based Plans: Define your desires not just in the immediate sense but also for the long term—1 year, 10 years, 20 years, and up to the end of your life. This long-term view helps maintain a clear direction and fosters a deeper connection with your path to abundance.

Incorporating the Exercise Practices

The exercises, such as the goal-setting exercise and crafting a list of 100 aspirations, are tools to aid in this realignment process. They provide a structured approach to clarifying your desires, communicating with the universe, and taking actionable steps toward your goals. Engaging with these exercises reignites the manifestation process, reaffirming your commitment to your journey toward abundance.

Finding your way back to abundance is a journey of rediscovery, requiring you to identify where you veered off your path, understand the causes, and take deliberate steps to realign with your goals and intentions. This process is not just about returning to where you left off but about deepening your understanding of the manifestation process and refining your approach to co-creation with the universe. It's a reminder that the path to abundance is always within reach, waiting for you to take the steps back to alignment, clarity, and purposeful action.

The Bucket List as a Map to Manifestation

The Bucket List as a Map to Manifestation transforms the concept of a bucket list from a mere compilation of dreams and desires into a strategic and intentional map for manifestation. In this context, the bucket list becomes more than a list of goals to achieve before a certain age or life milestone; it becomes a tool for deliberate creation, guiding your journey toward realizing your deepest aspirations and living a life aligned with your true purpose and joy.

Creating Your Manifestation Map

- Identify Core Desires: Start by identifying the experiences, achievements, and milestones that resonate deeply with you. These should be desires that stir your soul, contribute to your growth, and bring you profound joy and fulfillment.

- Prioritize with Purpose: Organize your list by what you want to do first and what will bring you closer to your higher self. Prioritize items with significant potential for personal growth, happiness, and contribution to others.

- Infuse with Intention: Set a clear and powerful intention for each item on your bucket list. Why do you want to achieve this? How will it serve you and others? What greater purpose does it fulfill? This intention-setting turns each goal into a beacon, attracting the necessary resources, opportunities, and alignments.

Navigating Your Manifestation Journey

- Visualize and Embody: Regularly visualize yourself achieving the items on your bucket list. More importantly, embody the feelings and energies associated with each accomplishment. This practice aligns your vibration with your desires, making manifestation more fluid.
- Action Steps: Break down each bucket list item into actionable steps. What can you do now to move closer to this goal? Even small actions can create momentum and signal your commitment to the universe.
- Flexibility and Flow: While having a clear map is essential, so is flexibility. Be open to the journey,

taking unexpected turns, and understand that sometimes the detours lead to even richer experiences than originally planned.

The Bucket List as a Living Document

- Review and Revise: Your bucket list is a living document reflecting your growth, experiences, and changing desires. Regularly review and update your list, adding new goals as you discover them and revisiting the intentions behind existing ones.
- Celebrate Achievements: Marking off completed items is a celebration of your co-creative power and the universe's responsiveness. Take time to honor each achievement, reflecting on the journey and lessons learned.
- Incorporate Gratitude: Gratitude amplifies the power of your bucket list. Be grateful for the dreams already realized and for those still in the process of manifestation. Gratitude keeps the heart open and receptive to the abundance of the universe.

The Bucket List as a Map to Manifestation elevates the concept of a bucket list from a series of unchecked desires to a dynamic tool for intentional living and manifestation. By crafting your list with purpose, navigating your journey with action and flexibility, and continuously aligning your goals with your evolving self, you turn your bucket list into a powerful manifestation map. This approach brings you closer to achieving your individual goals and aligns your life path with your deepest values, contributing to a fulfilling and purpose-driven existence.

Goal setting is a powerful process for thinking about your ideal future and for motivating yourself to turn your vision of this future into reality. It involves the development of an action plan designed to motivate and guide you toward a desired outcome. Proper goal setting allows you to focus your efforts, use your time and resources productively, and increase your chances of achieving what you want in life.

Understanding Goal Setting

- Clarity: Effective goals are clear and specific. This makes it easier to focus on what you want to achieve and helps prevent any confusion along the way. A well-defined goal should answer the what, why, and how of your aspirations.

- Measurability: Goals should be measurable so that you can track your progress. This provides motivation and allows for adjustments to be made as needed. Setting measurable goals answers the question of how much, how many, and how will I know when the goal is accomplished.

- Attainability: While goals should be challenging, they also need to be realistic and attainable. Setting impossible goals only sets you up for failure. By setting achievable goals, you ensure that you're pushing yourself, but not so far that the goal becomes unattainable.

- Relevance: Goals need to be relevant to your life and the direction you want it to take. This means setting goals that align with your values, long-term objectives, and current circumstances.

- Time-bound: Effective goals have a clearly defined timeline, including a starting point and a target end date. This creates a sense of urgency and prompts action.

The Importance of Goal Setting

- Direction: Clear goals give you direction and focus. Without them, you can spend a lot of time doing a lot of things without actually achieving anything meaningful.
- Motivation: Setting a goal provides the motivation needed to achieve what you desire. It helps turn abstract desires into concrete targets with actionable steps.
- Overcoming Procrastination: Goals with set deadlines force you to organize and take action instead of putting off tasks to a later date.
- Personal Satisfaction: Achieving your goals brings a sense of accomplishment and satisfaction. This success boosts your self-confidence and provides encouragement to set and achieve more goals.

Strategies for Effective Goal Setting

- Write Down Your Goals: **Writing down your goals increases your commitment and helps you clarify what you truly want to achieve.**

- Set SMART Goals: **Ensure your goals are Specific, Measurable, Achievable, Relevant, and Time-bound.**

- Create an Action Plan: **Break down your goal into smaller, manageable tasks and set short-term milestones. This makes it easier to manage and less overwhelming.**

- Visualize Your Success: **Spend time visualizing and achieving your goal. This positive reinforcement strengthens your commitment and keeps you focused.**

- Review and Adjust: Regularly review your progress toward your goals. Be prepared to adjust your action plan as needed to stay on track.

Goal setting is identifying what you want to achieve and giving yourself the means to ensure you follow through. By setting clearly defined goals, you can measure your progress and take pride in your achievements. This forward momentum can help you overcome obstacles and make your dreams and desires a reality.

Your Plan

Imagine a solitary dot on a whiteboard, representing you at the start of your journey toward abundance and fulfillment. Without a plan, goals, or aspirations, this dot's potential paths are numerous and chaotic, radiating out in all directions without focus or destination. This represents life without a clear plan—actions and decisions are made, but they lack coherence and direction, making it challenging for the universe or spirit to understand and support your true desires. In this scenario, the flow of life is erratic, unpredictable, and often unfulfilling because it lacks intention and purpose.

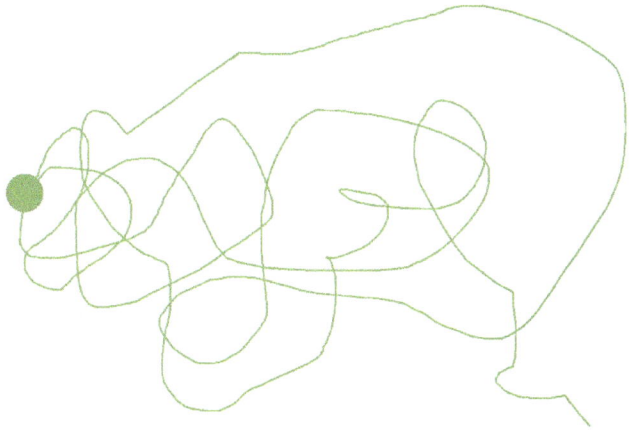

Now, envision drawing a straight line from that dot, marked with intervals labeled "1 Year," "5 Years," "10 Years," and so on, extending all the way to "End of Life." This line transforms the chaotic potential into a directed path, a visual representation of setting time-based plans. Each point on the line signifies a milestone, a checkpoint of sorts, where specific goals and aspirations are meant to be realized. This structure provides a clear, focused direction for your energy and intentions, making it significantly easier for the universe or spirit to align with your desires and assist in their manifestation.

By informing the universe of your timeline and specific goals at each interval, you create a synergy between your desires and the cosmic forces that help bring them to fruition. It's like providing a map to a treasure hunter; the journey becomes more efficient with clear directions, and the likelihood of finding treasure increases exponentially.

This straight line, marked with your planned milestones, symbolizes a life lived with intention, purpose, and clarity. It illustrates the power of setting time-based plans, allowing for a more focused and directed effort toward achieving your goals. With this approach, you make it easier for yourself to gauge progress and adjust strategies and enable the universe or spirit to provide support, guidance, and opportunities aligned with your path to abundance.

The transition from a dot with chaotic potential to a clearly marked path embodies the transformation from aimlessness to purpose-driven living. It highlights the importance of planning, setting goals, and having aspirations that stretch throughout the entirety of your life. This strategic approach to life ensures that every action taken is a step toward the realization of your deepest desires, with the universe as your ally, guiding and aiding you along the way.

Remember to create a new plan right up until death(you can always update the plan)!

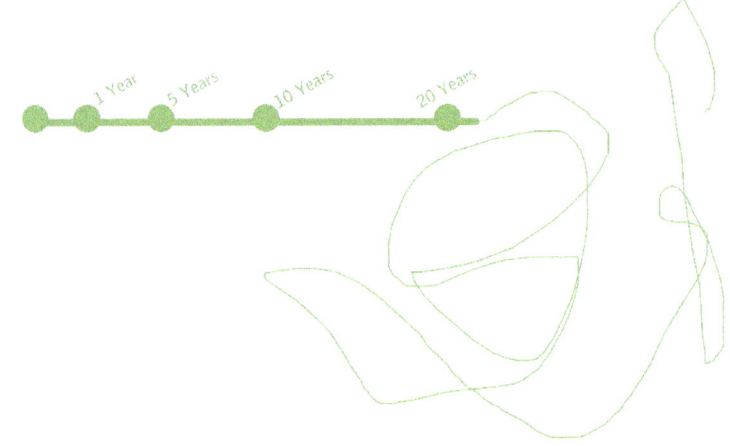

Exercise #1:

Crafting a List of 100 Aspirations (Goals)

Task yourself with jotting down a comprehensive list of 100 aspirations or items for your bucket list, not merely ten or fifty but a total of 100.

Regardless of whether you think these goals are within your reach, the act of writing them is crucial. It's said that putting pen to paper and articulating your dreams can alter your brain's chemistry, setting the stage for your reality to unfold.

Consider how your perception shifts with the cars you drive. Initially, you might notice every vehicle identical to yours on the streets. Switch cars, and suddenly, your attention shifts to the new model, leaving the old one a distant memory. This phenomenon underscores the incredible selective attention of our brains, akin to the law of attraction: we draw toward us what occupies our thoughts.

For your list, here are some prompts to ignite your imagination:

- Destinations you'd love to explore—each destination counts.
- The ideal home you envision.
- Furniture that reflects your style.
- Gadgets and toys you desire.
- Achievements you aim for.
- Hobbies you wish to pursue.
- Volunteer work that calls to you.
- Opportunities for public speaking.
- Thrill-seeking activities like bungee jumping or skydiving. Anything that sparks your interest is worth noting. Allow yourself weeks if needed; there's no rush. Feel free to expand your list as you accomplish items or as new aspirations emerge.

Many who undertake this exercise find themselves achieving over eighty percent of their listed goals, often noticing a shift in their reality almost immediately.

This approach is adaptable for any specific goal:

- For home renovations: detail the modifications desired for each room.

- For career aspirations, note the job type, salary, and position.
- For planning a trip, outline the specifics.

Before beginning, it's wise to establish certain principles with the universe, God, or whatever higher power you believe in, ensuring that your pursuit of these goals will not:

- Leading to financial ruin.
- Cause relationship breakdowns.
- Negatively impact your family life or interfere with existing priorities.

Once you've penned down your dreams, desires, and wishes, the next step is to identify and overcome any barriers holding you back. The subsequent sections will offer strategies for clearing away these obstacles and actualizing your dreams!

Exercise #2:

Crafting Your Ideal Partner Blueprint

To manifest your ideal partner, it's essential to articulate precisely what qualities, characteristics, and life circumstances you seek in them. Embarking on this exercise of listing 100 detailed attributes you desire in a perfect mate can significantly enhance the clarity of your intentions, drawing you closer to attracting the relationship that aligns with your deepest values and desires.

Application Rule

After dating someone for at least three months, evaluate your relationship against your list. If they match at least 80% of your criteria, they're likely a good fit. If not, it may be wise to reconsider the relationship. Life is too brief to compromise on fundamental aspects of your partner that ensure happiness and fulfillment.

Reminder

Society, family, or religious guilt often makes it difficult to leave a relationship once deeply involved. Hence, it's prudent to know exactly what you're looking for before making significant commitments. Doing your "homework" upfront can save you from the pain of realizing later that you've chosen a path that isn't right for you. This exercise isn't just about attracting the right partner; it's about creating a foundation for a relationship that brings out the best in both individuals, fostering growth, happiness, and mutual respect.

- Physical Appearance: Delve into specifics such as hair color, eye color, height, weight, and style of dress. These physical attributes, while not the essence of a person, contribute to your initial attraction and compatibility.
- Desire for Children: Clearly state your preferences regarding children, including whether you want them and how many, as these are pivotal life decisions that affect long-term compatibility.
- Hobbies and Interests: Identify hobbies that are important to you, whether it's art, reading, gaming, sports, or watching movies. Sharing common interests can strengthen your bond.
- Political and Social Views: Compatibility in political and social beliefs can be crucial for some individuals. Specify the importance of shared views in these areas.
- Career and Lifestyle: Consider their job, income level, willingness to travel, and whether it matters if you work. Aligning on career and lifestyle choices can prevent future conflicts.

- Family Dynamics: **Express your preferences regarding family interactions, including the relationship with in-laws and the role of family in your lives.**

- Habits and Addictions: **Be clear about your stance on smoking, drug use, alcohol consumption, eating habits, and gambling. Such habits can significantly impact relationship dynamics.**

- Sexual Compatibility: **Sexual compatibility is a key aspect of a fulfilling relationship for many. Consider including your needs and preferences in this area.**

- Shared Experiences: **Think about how you want to spend your holidays, the types of trips you enjoy, and general lifestyle choices, such as how you both drive or your attitudes toward punctuality.**

- Financial Management: **Discuss attitudes toward spending, saving, and planning for retirement. Financial harmony is crucial for a stress-free relationship.**

- Values and Ethics: **The importance of honesty, integrity, and the amount of time spent together reflects your core values in a relationship.**

- Social Life: Consider how your ideal mate interacts with friends, your expectations around socializing together, and separately.
- Living Arrangements: Where you live—be it the location or type of residence—plays a significant role in your daily life and happiness.

Exercise #3:

This exercise is designed to delve into the depths of your desires and the obstacles that may be hindering your progress toward achieving your dreams or goals. By addressing these questions, you gain insights into what drives you, what holds you back, and how your current life context may influence your aspirations. Let's break down each question to help you navigate through the introspection process.

Understanding the Drive Behind Your Goal

- What will you gain from achieving your goal? Consider the outcomes, both tangible and intangible. This could include personal fulfillment, financial stability, improved health, or deeper relationships. Identifying what you stand to gain can clarify the value and purpose behind your goal.

Identifying Current Obstacles

- What stops you from achieving your dream today? Pinpoint the barriers currently in your way. These could be practical issues, such as financial constraints, lack of time, or need for education, or psychological barriers like fear, procrastination, or low self-esteem.

Considering the Impact

- If you achieved your dream, what or who would it negatively affect? Acknowledge any potential negative outcomes of achieving your goal. This can include the effect on family dynamics, current job situation, or even lifestyle changes that may not be entirely positive. Recognizing these aspects can help you prepare for or mitigate unwanted consequences.

Aligning Goals with Current Life

- How will your present situation, behaviors, and beliefs affect your 100 goals? Reflect on how your current life circumstances and mindset support or hinder your goals. For example, a desire to travel extensively might clash with family responsibilities or a career that demands your physical presence.

Emotional Response to Setbacks

- What do you feel when you don't achieve your goal? Identifying the emotions associated with setbacks or failure—be it frustration, sadness, or indifference—can offer insights into your level of attachment to the goal and what adjustments might be necessary to maintain motivation.

Moving Forward with Insight

- Having answered these questions, patterns in your responses may reveal underlying reasons or "excuses" that have prevented you from reaching your goals. Understanding these patterns is the first step in overcoming them. It's essential to confront and acknowledge these barriers to pave the way for progress.

Exercise #4: Decision-Making Insights

The coin-flip technique mentioned highlights the importance of listening to your intuitive, emotional response rather than the outcome itself. This instinctive reaction can serve as a guide, helping you align your decisions with your true feelings and desires. If a particular outcome causes disappointment or relief, it's a sign to reevaluate your choices based on those internal cues rather than on chance or external pressures.

This introspective exercise is a powerful tool for self-discovery and overcoming the hurdles that stand in the way of your dreams. By honestly addressing these questions, you can identify what truly matters, understand the obstacles you face, and navigate your path toward achieving your goals with greater awareness and alignment with your deepest values and desires.

Exercise #5: Guided Relaxation Meditation

This meditation is a tool not just for relaxation but for self-discovery and emotional cleansing, aiding in the manifestation of your deepest desires by aligning your body, mind, and spirit in harmony and clarity.

This meditation is designed to be recorded or spoken to you, providing a tranquil experience, ideally before sleep or during a calming bath. Use a gentle, soothing tone, pausing briefly at each ellipsis before continuing to the next phrase.

Finding Comfort and Breath Awareness

Find a comfortable position, allowing your body to relax fully.

- Begin by focusing on your breath. Notice its natural rhythm as you inhale and exhale. Feel the air moving in and out...
- Observe the length of each breath, feeling the gentle pause between inhalation and exhalation...
- With each breath, imagine releasing any tension or negative energy from your body...

- Shift your awareness to your toes. You might gently wiggle them, acknowledging their presence...

- Breathe deeply, directing the breath to your toes, releasing any discomfort or negativity...

- Move your attention to your ankles. Allow any held tension to dissolve away...

- Gradually, let this sensation of release move up to your calves, knees, and then to your thighs, letting go of negativity with each breath...

- Focus on your hips, then slowly up through your torso, allowing each breath to release any stored negativity or pain...

- Pay attention to your shoulders, arms, hands, and fingers, encouraging a sense of release with every exhale...

- Notice your neck and head. With each breath, ease any tension within your neck, face, cheeks, lips, eyes, ears, and nose...

Deepening Mental Relaxation

- Having relaxed your body, turn inward to calm your mind...
- Start to count down slowly from 100 in your mind. With each number, sink deeper into relaxation...
- Allow the numbers to fade away after 97, finding yourself in a state of deep peace...

Releasing Negativity

- Imagine a box with a lockable lid before you. Visualize placing any lingering negative thoughts, feelings, or sensations into this box...
- Once all negativity is contained, close the lid and lock it. Decide whether to keep this box stored or let it vanish entirely. The choice is yours...

A Journey to Relaxation

- Now, envision yourself transported to a serene setting, resting in a comfortable hammock or lounge chair, the weather perfect, just as you like it...

- Allow yourself to drift into pleasant daydreams, feeling the comfort and peace of the moment...
- As you bask in this tranquility, gently begin to return awareness to your body. Notice your toes, giving them a small wiggle, awakening from relaxation...
- Stretch gently, opening your eyes when ready, feeling refreshed and rejuvenated.

For Deeper Insights

If seeking a deeper understanding of unfulfilled desires in this serene setting, ask yourself: "What do I need to know or understand? What's blocking my dreams or desires from manifesting?"

Remain open to any insights, feelings, or images that arise, knowing this peaceful space can offer clarity and guidance.

Conclusion: The Path
Manifested

As we journey through the pages of this exploration, we traverse the rich landscape of manifestation, uncovering the nuanced dynamics between our deepest selves and the expansive universe. This journey is more than a simple pursuit of desires; it's an invitation to engage deeply with the fabric of our being and the cosmic forces that animate our existence. Through understanding manifestation, confronting and overcoming personal barriers, and learning to communicate effectively with the universe, we embark on a path of profound personal and spiritual development.

The essence of this exploration emphasizes the critical importance of clarity, action, and emotional intelligence in the manifestation process. Clarity acts as the beacon, guiding our desires through the tumultuous seas of possibility into the harbor of reality. Without clarity, our desires remain nebulous dreams, floating aimlessly in the realm of potential. Clarity sharpens our focus, directing our energies toward the manifestation of our truest intentions.

Action serves as the vehicle through which our desires transition from the ethereal to the tangible. It is through action that we engage with the universe, signaling our readiness and willingness to co-create the reality we envision. Each step taken is a declaration of our commitment to the path we choose to manifest, imbued with the power of our intention and the depth of our desire.

Emotional intelligence provides the insight and adaptability needed to navigate the manifestation process. It enables us to understand and manage our emotions, aligning them with our desires to create a powerful resonance that attracts corresponding energies from the universe. Emotional intelligence also fosters resilience, allowing us to navigate setbacks and challenges with grace, learning from each experience and emerging stronger and more aligned with our path.

This journey through manifestation is not linear but a spiral, ever-evolving and expanding as we grow and transform. It invites us to delve into the depths of our being, to uncover and release the blockages that hinder our path, and to embrace the limitless potential that lies within. As we align our intentions with our actions and harmonize our emotions with our desires, we co-create with the universe, weaving the fabric of our reality into a tapestry of abundance, fulfillment, and profound spiritual awakening.

In conclusion, the path manifested is a testament to the power of the human spirit, the boundless generosity of the universe, and the magical interplay between the two. It is a reminder that within each of us lies the potential to shape our destiny, transform our dreams into reality, and embark on a journey of deep and lasting transformation. As we close this chapter, let us step forward with renewed purpose, emboldened by the knowledge that the path to manifestation is ours to walk, guided by the light of our clarity, the strength of our actions, and the wisdom of our emotional intelligence. The journey continues, and with each step, we manifest the abundance and joy that is our birthright.

Bibliography

Foundational Texts

- Jung, Carl. The Archetypes and The Collective Unconscious. Princeton University Press, 1981.
- Proctor, Bob, and Greg S. Reid. Think and Grow Rich: A Black Choice. Ballantine Books, 1997.
- Erikson, Erik H. Identity and the Life Cycle. W. W. Norton & Company, 1994.
- Dyer, Wayne. Wishes Fulfilled: Mastering the Art of Manifesting. Hay House Inc., 2012.

Spirituality and Healing

- Hay, Louise L. You Can Heal Your Life. Hay House Inc., 1984.
- Myss, Caroline. Anatomy of the Spirit: The Seven Stages of Power and Healing. Harmony, 1996.

- Tolle, Eckhart. The Power of Now: A Guide to Spiritual Enlightenment. New World Library, 1999.

Law of Attraction and Manifestation

- Byrne, Rhonda. The Secret. Atria Books/Beyond Words, 2006.
- Hicks, Esther, and Jerry Hicks. Ask and It Is Given: Learning to Manifest Your Desires. Hay House Inc., 2004.
- Dooley, Mike. Infinite Possibilities: The Art of Living Your Dreams. Atria Books/Beyond Words, 2009.

Energy Work and Consciousness

- Braden, Gregg. The Divine Matrix: Bridging Time, Space, Miracles, and Belief. Hay House Inc., 2007.
- Dispenza, Joe. Becoming Supernatural: How Common People Are Doing the Uncommon. Hay House Inc., 2017.
- Lipton, Bruce H. The Biology of Belief: Unleashing the Power of Consciousness, Matter & Miracles. Hay House Inc., 2008.

Personal Development and Growth

- Brown, Brené. The Gifts of Imperfection: Let Go of Who You Think You're Supposed to Be and Embrace Who You Are. Hazelden Publishing, 2010.
- Covey, Stephen R. The 7 Habits of Highly Effective People: Powerful Lessons in Personal Change. Simon & Schuster, 1989.
- Ruiz, Don Miguel. The Four Agreements: A Practical Guide to Personal Freedom (A Toltec Wisdom Book). Amber-Allen Publishing, 1997.

Acknowledgments

In the journey of crafting Bend, Don't Break: Finding Your Way Back to Abundance, I have been graced with the support, wisdom, and encouragement of countless individuals whose contributions have been instrumental in bringing this work to life. This page is a humble attempt to extend my heartfelt gratitude to those who have been part of this journey.

First and foremost, I wish to express my deepest appreciation to my family, whose unwavering love and support have been my constant source of strength and inspiration. Your belief in my vision has been a beacon of light on my path, illuminating the way through moments of doubt and uncertainty.

To my mentors and teachers, both seen and unseen, who have guided me through the intricate landscapes of spirituality, psychology, and personal development—your teachings have been the foundation upon which this book rests. Your wisdom has shaped my understanding and approach to the art of manifestation, and for that, I am eternally grateful.

A special note of thanks to the pioneers of thought in the realms of natural medicine, energy work, and the law of attraction. The works of Carl Jung, Bob Proctor, Wayne Dyer, and Louise Hay, among others, have been invaluable resources that have informed and enriched the content of this book. Your contributions to the collective understanding of human potential and healing have paved the way for a new era of personal transformation.

I am profoundly thankful to my spiritual community and peers, whose shared experiences and insights have added depth and authenticity to this work. Your stories of resilience, growth, and abundance have been a wellspring of inspiration, reminding me of the transformative power of aligning with our highest selves.

To my editor and the publishing team, whose expertise and dedication have shaped this manuscript into the book it is today—I am immensely appreciative of your patience, guidance, and commitment to excellence. Your contributions have been pivotal in ensuring that this work reaches those who seek guidance on their path to abundance.

A heartfelt thank you to the readers and seekers of truth who have embarked on this journey with me. Your quest for understanding, healing, and fulfillment is the reason this book exists. May the pages of this book serve as a companion on your journey, offering insights, encouragement, and clarity as you navigate the path to manifesting your desires.

Finally, I extend my gratitude to the universe for its endless guidance, synchronicities, and support. The process of writing this book has been a manifestation in itself, a testament to the principles it explores. May we all continue to bend without breaking, finding our way back to the abundance that is our birthright.

With love and light, Dr. Constance Santego

Message from the

Message from the

Author

Author

Dear Readers,

As you've journeyed through these pages, you've encountered a fundamental truth underpinning much of what we've explored: the power of thought in shaping reality. The old adage "Be careful what you wish for. You just might get it" rings especially true in the art of manifestation. It's a gentle reminder that our desires, framed by our thoughts and intentions, hold the potential to unfold into our reality. The essence of your question, your intent, is the cornerstone of this process. Crafting the question is the initial step; receiving the answer, though seemingly complex, flows with ease once the question is clear and intentioned.

Now, the journey toward trusting yourself is a personal and inward one. It's about building confidence in your intuition and the signals the universe sends you in response to your queries. This trust doesn't emerge overnight. Rather, it's cultivated through continuous practice and reflection—testing and retesting your inner guidance until it becomes second nature. When you reach a point where you can pose a question and embrace the answer with unwavering confidence, you'll know you're on the right path, taking the perfect next action for your journey.

Cultivating such a habit is all about persistence. Practice, practice, and then practice some more. To shift a paradigm, as Bob Proctor insightfully teaches, there are predominantly two avenues: relentless practice or an experience so profound—be it traumatic or extraordinarily positive—that it instantly transforms our perspective. Most of us prefer the gradual path, one marked by diligent, ongoing practice, allowing us to slowly but surely realign our paradigms in a more manageable, less tumultuous manner.

This process of continuous practice isn't just about achieving mastery over our thoughts and manifesting our desires. It's also a journey of self-discovery, of delving deep into our inner worlds to uncover, understand, and eventually trust the profound wisdom that resides within. As you walk this path, remember that each step, each practice session, is a building block toward a more aligned, intuitive, and empowered self.

In closing, my hope is that these insights serve not only as a guide to manifesting the life you envision but also as an invitation to trust in your own profound capacity to shape your reality. Trust in yourself, in the practice, and in the journey. Your path to manifestation is uniquely yours, and I'm here cheering you on every step of the way.

With warmth and belief in your journey, Dr. Constance

About the Author

Dr. Constance Santego is a luminary in the fields of personal development and spiritual growth, guiding individuals back to a path of abundance and self-realization. Her latest work, Bend, Don't Break: Finding Your Way Back to Abundance, encapsulates her lifelong dedication to merging the realms of practical life skills with profound spiritual insights.

With a background enriched by diverse experiences in healing, teaching, and guiding, Constance has carved a unique niche that blends the essence of traditional wisdom with contemporary practices. Her approach to life and healing is holistic, focusing on the symptoms and the root causes of disconnection and discontent. This perspective has illuminated her path as an educator, healer, and author, making her a beacon for those lost in the complexity of modern life and seeking a way back to their true essence.

Connstance's journey into the world of healing and spiritual guidance began early, fueled by a relentless quest for knowledge and the desire to understand the underpinnings of human potential. Her academic pursuits led her to explore the depths of Natural Medicine, earning her credentials that include a doctorate in this field and certifications as a Reiki Master, Educator, Life Coach, and Spiritual Guide. Each title she holds is a testament to her unwavering commitment to helping others achieve wellness, balance, and fulfillment.

Through her books, Dr. Santego invites readers into a world where love, life, and enlightenment converge, offering insights that spark transformation and healing. Bend, Don't Break is more than a book; it's a journey that encourages readers to rediscover their power, realign with their desires, and manifest the life of abundance they are destined for. Her writing is an extension of her knowledge and a reflection of her belief in the transformative power of blending ancient wisdom with modern insights.

Constance's influence extends beyond her written work into the holistic health and wellness school she founded, which has become a sanctuary for those seeking to deepen their understanding of themselves and the world around them. Here, students are equipped with the knowledge and tools necessary for personal growth, healing, and the ability to assist others on their journey.

In her latest exploration, Bend, Don't Break: Finding Your Way Back to Abundance," co-authored with ChatGPT, Dr. Constance Santego offers a beacon of hope and a map for navigating the complexities of life with grace and resilience. Her work is an open invitation to embark on a transformative journey guided by the light of understanding, compassion, and the unwavering belief in the potential that lies within us all.

To dive deeper into Connie Santego's teachings, discover her insights, and embark on your own journey of transformation, visit www.constancesantego.ca. Here, at the crossroads of healing and wisdom, a world of transformative learning awaits.

Discover More

Embark on an Adventure with "Ikona – Discover Your Inner Genie"

Dive deeper into the world of empowerment and self-discovery with a range of offerings designed to inspire and transform. Explore the full spectrum of Constance Santego's motivational products, personalized coaching sessions, spiritual retreats, engaging live events, and enriching educational programs.

- Connect, Learn, and Grow:
- Website: Journey further into our resources and offerings at www.ConstanceSantego.ca.
- Instagram: Join our community @Constance_Santego for daily inspiration and insights.
- Facebook: Stay updated with the latest events and connect with like-minded individuals on Constance Santego's Facebook Page.

- YouTube: Subscribe to Constance Santego's YouTube Channel for free resources, meditations, and more to guide you on your path to self-improvement.

Your journey toward personal growth and enlightenment is just a click away. Discover the tools and support you need to unlock your potential and manifest your dreams.

Bend, Don't Break: Finding Your Way Back To Abundance 271

www.ingramcontent.com/pod-product-compliance
Lightning Source LLC
Chambersburg PA
CBHW070910120626
46546CB00001B/209